Travel for Two

The Art of Compromise

Travel for Two
The Art of Compromise

Margot S. Biestman

Pèrgot Press
Sausalito, California

First Printing 1986

Printed in the United States of America

Illustrations by Margot S. Biestman
Maps by Jay Smith
Cover by Anne Biestman
Design and Production by Marilyn Mansfield
Set in Meridien by The Compleat Works

Library of Congress Cataloging in Publication Data

Biestman, Margot S., 1931–
Travel for two – the art of compromise.

Bibliography: p.
Includes index.
1. Travel. I. Title.
G51.B54 1986 910'.2'02 86-60222
ISBN 0-936865-07-5

Pèrgot Press
1001 J Bridgeway, Suite 227
Sausalito, California 94965

To Perry,

my partner in the art of compromise—

with love,

and

in celebration of our travels together

Contents

Preface

My husband and I began thinking about this book ten years ago while traveling in Greece. I was standing high up on a plateau in the shadow of an austere Albanian mountain near the village of Monodendri, when I read aloud that morning's entry from my journal:

> The rain was pouring down, with thunder and lightning. The car's windshield wiper on the driver's side suddenly flew off and I was panic-stricken at the view from my side window: sheer drops off the cliff. We had to stop frequently in the middle of the narrow mountain road because we couldn't see anything at all. When we finally arrived in Monodendri I burst into tears of relief, hugged Perry, and said he deserved a reward.
>
> What were we doing on such a road in that kind of weather? Why Monodendri? The atmosphere was eerie—cold and stark. Perry had wanted to see the monastery, which friends had said resembled those in Tibet.
>
> When the rain let up we walked to that monastery, beside lush green grass to the left of us, filled with pinks, red poppies, white lacelike flowers, blue muscari, and wild bachelor buttons. To the right were steep precipices. A monastery constructed of cold gray slate stood at the end of the narrow trail, its door open; we entered as if compelled by a mystery. From inside we heard the sound of bells and could hardly believe what we saw from the courtyard across the ravine. Climbing from far, far below were goats, who were somehow able to walk on the fraction of earth at the edge of the cliffs. I imagined despots throwing their enemies off into these ravines. I felt I couldn't breathe along the entire walk, until we returned to the slate gray village. I had never seen

this kind of mountain world before, the contrast of the flowers' warmth and the icy cold cliffs. Would we ever get back down the mountain? What if the rainstorm let loose again? Fear seems to me too high a price to pay for this kind of excitement, but Perry said he wouldn't have missed it for anything and would love to do it again.

We just stared at one another and shook our heads in disagreement. We had a problem and didn't know how to solve it.

"You write so well," Perry said, "that you should write a book." We laughed lightly, but I liked what Perry said and tucked the idea away and hugged it to myself.

My writing and Perry's appreciation of it that day was the beginning of this book as well as our continued dedication to the art of decision-making—a study that would enrich every aspect of our lives. There at Monodendri we realized the extent of our opposing needs and desires. At the time we felt helpless about resolving our differences, which seemed to come with us wherever we went.

During the next few years we developed skills and learned techniques for making satisfying decisions, not only at home but also when we traveled. On the following trips each of us kept a daily journal and we read aloud to one another in the evenings. One day Perry suggested that I write a travel book about the special way we took trips. We began to talk about how extensively we'd traveled throughout this country, Europe, North and Central America, and the Far East—and how, after thirty-four years of marriage, we'd developed a real team approach to vacation and travel. With excitement we discussed a book that would build upon my having taught interpersonal problem-solving skills to people of many different ages, backgrounds, and experiences—complemented by Perry's knowledge of travel resources and special skills in planning. We wanted to share with fellow travelers—both close to home and far away—techniques we'd tried to alleviate the travel stress we'd experienced on our earlier trips.

Vacation and Travel Stress

Vacation and travel can prove more stressful than relaxing because of the difficulties posed by unfamiliar surroundings; change of schedule and pace; unusual food, customs, or accommodations; bad weather and plane delays; or problems created by financial concerns, tensions, and unrealistic expectations.

Dr. Herbert Peterson, Department of Psychiatry, University of California, San Francisco, explains:

> Leisure time on vacation, when ordinary limits are removed, is particularly difficult. Many people don't realize this as a problem until they are on vacation and wonder why they are not enjoying it. An increase in quarrels is one manifestation of the anxiety generated by this situation. Although people may resent the structure that defines their life on the job and at home, when it is taken away, they are lost. For this reason, some people enjoy travel more than a leisure vacation because it creates an artificial structure. For others it is more difficult. An individual traveling alone may find his or her situation lonely, yet on the other hand, loneliness can be even more intense with a partner who also does not know how to cope with travel or vacation stress.

Audience

The book is designed for people who want to travel with a partner with as much comfort and pleasure as possible while exploring new horizons. The suggestions and techniques can be used by any pair of partners—married or single, of the same or opposite sex, experienced or inexperienced travelers—regardless of age, destination, or budget.

Specifically, this book is for those of you who:

- have previously taken vacations together and been dissatisfied;
- want to make your good times traveling even better;
- have not yet gone on a trip with a partner and would like to try it; or
- want to explore the art of making compromises and learn techniques that you can also apply to your everyday lives.

This is a self-help book that illustrates how you might add pleasure and reduce some of the pain of travel, and how you might spend from two weeks to a month with a partner and end up liking him or her more than before the trip began. The book also helps explode some of this country's cultural assumptions about the "ideal traveler" such as:

- You must see as much as you can and take advantage of every golden opportunity.

- You must have energy at all times, never be tired.
- You must be different from who you are at home: you must always be in a good mood and never lose your temper, you must leave your disagreements behind and forget all your worries.
- You must relax; if you have to work at planning a vacation something must be "wrong."
- You and your partner must be together all the time to achieve the All-American dream. If either of you wants to spend time alone you must not have a very good relationship.

Throughout the book questions are posed—not as a burden or "heavy duty" homework, but rather as a guide to help you and your partner plan a trip that will meet your individual needs and desires by caring for your idiosyncrasies (rather than belittling yourselves for having them) and developing techniques for making compromises in areas of disagreement. If you choose, your trip can become a journey during which you develop skills adaptable to daily living at home.

Acknowledgments

After organizing material from Perry's and my travel journals, I wrote and edited. During the first year I met weekly to read aloud and edit my manuscript with my friends and teaching colleagues, Anne Smith and Joan Dodd (who is also my sister). I also met weekly with Katherine Crowe, teacher and author, to read and edit once again. On weekends I met with Perry to review and modify even further. Sharing my work along the way reduced my sense of loneliness in the art of writing and increased my confidence to continue.

At the end of a year I met with Amy Einsohn, a freelance editor, who encouraged me in my ideas, proposed changes in organization of material, and provided careful, considered, and often humorous editing comments throughout several versions of the manuscript. I met frequently with Juanita Sagan, Director of the Institute for Creative and Artistic Development, my educational consultant, teacher, and dear friend of many years. Juanita and her husband Eugene had also developed the Creative Behavior Process for solving problems, which I've used throughout the book. Dr. Herbert Peterson, University of California Medical Center, read the manuscript and enthusiastically offered useful suggestions based on his knowledge of human relationships. Dr. Gerald Redwine helped me to recognize my accomplishments and enjoy the fruits of my labor. Our daughter-in-law, Karen Williams Biestman, a faculty member at the University of California at Berkeley, reviewed and critiqued my work. In addition, I received commentaries from Lisa Hunter, a project director at Far West Laboratory for Educational Research and Development. Members of the writers' class at the Institute for Creative and Artistic Development gave consistent encouragement while offering constructive criticism. I am particularly grateful for the attentive listening and comments by Marilyn Jensen, Mark Brucker, and Sara Somers, as well as the many fellow travelers of all ages who shared their stories and answered questions in my interviews. I appreciated assistance and expressions of pride along the way from our three children, John, Mark, and Anne; our daughters-in-law, Lori and Karen; and Nell Sinton, my mother, a professional artist.

I give these people, so important in our lives, my thanks for their support, affection, and hard work to make this book a celebration.

1

Deciding to Travel

"I simply can't stand it!" my mother screamed, "I simply can't stand it another minute!" The plane that was to take her and my father from Calcutta to Bangkok—the plane they had pulled themselves out of bed at 5:00 a.m. to catch—was simply not going to land to pick them up, and no one at the airport would explain why. My father tore around the airline ticket counters, white from the heat, dragging baggage, determined to maneuver his way through the red tape or have a tantrum himself. When my mother shrieked for the third time, "I can't STAND it!", a mild-mannered man standing next to her asked with deliberate quiet and condescension, "Lady, why do you travel?"

WHY TRAVEL?

My mother was shocked to her senses immediately. "If you travel," she told me many years later, "you have to expect that anything can happen, anything bad and anything good, whether you are in Calcutta or at a campground an hour away from home. When you're traveling you have to expect the unexpected."

Why DO we travel? For many reasons: to satisfy our curiosity or visit a relative or friend, to celebrate an accomplishment or explore a place we've read about, to rest and gather new ideas, or to impress friends or relatives. And sometimes we're not sure just why we're traveling—to escape our problems or to gain perspective on them?

I traveled.
I listened.
I changed.[1]

Knowing *why* you're going somewhere on vacation is as important as figuring out *where* to go. In addition to an itinerary of places to visit, you need a set of goals or purposes. Once you know *what* your reasons are, you also need to know if the purposes of your travels are *feasible* and *worthwhile to you*. For example, if you travel to impress your associates and friends or to gain parental approval, do you *really* accomplish that goal? Even if you do, is having a terrible time, seeing sights you don't care about, spending more than makes sense for your total budget worth the expense to you personally? If you really do enjoy many of the same activities as your colleagues or relatives, and can afford the trip, that is a different story. You are fortunate in meeting your goal as well as making it worth your while. Knowing *why* you travel gives you a focus for *what* to do when you're traveling, and a way of *evaluating* if you've done what you set out to do. If you know your reasons for travel in the past, you can choose to continue in the same way as before, or to make changes to fit your reasons for going now.

For example, in my twenties I traveled to win my family's approval. Although I didn't realize it then, I traveled to confirm my status as a cultured woman of the world. If my relatives were world travelers then I should be too. But since I wasn't clear about my purposes I didn't really enjoy my trips in themselves—they were acquisitions to show off to my family—and I used to rush about getting as cultured as I could as fast as possible. I hated myself (considered myself a "bad girl") if I was too tired to see the sights I "should" have been adding to my collection. Only later, when I understood my motives for traveling that way, was I able to plan vacations that met my deeper need and desire—to ramble slowly through the countryside with my husband.

How and why did the change come about in my new need to travel with a partner rather than alone? Traveling as a couple meant new demands which I did not consider at the time. Perry and I went through several stages of development of our purposes for travel: (1) my relatives' purpose for us; (2) my purpose for us (*my* way learned from my relatives); (3) Perry's purpose for us (*his* way); and (4) *our* purpose for us.

1. From a sermon by a minister of the Church of England.

At first I was lonely and wanted to share with Perry what I had learned from my relatives—that "good things in life are found through travel" and "one must have a good time." We traveled with the same purpose as my family. I had transferred their desires for me to *my* desires for us, and Perry wanted to find out what those "good things" were, and what a "good time" was like. We returned from our trips telling family what a "good time" we'd had without knowing our own definition of the term. Since we weren't yet strong enough in knowing our own values we fell easy prey to self-put downs if our opinions were different from relatives. Therefore, it was easier and safer to tell ourselves and family that we had had a good time rather than hearing disapproving voices, "*What*? You didn't like Stratford?" or feeling guilty because we hadn't gone to see a painting in a tiny church or a linen shop after six hours of sightseeing.

It took several years and three or four major trips to decide we had not been satisfied in the past when I had pushed to be "Mrs. Full-in-Charge," when I had made lists upon lists of things to do, see, eat, and buy. I'd made all the arrangements, had written letters to hotels, and awaited replies as if waiting to hear we'd been accepted into college. I was not happy after visiting twenty-five places in thirty days, having driven many miles, and neither of us was pleased in remembering that if we hadn't arrived at a place by the time we had figured out, we had thrown tantrums about not meeting our expectations. We didn't like not remembering much of what we had seen, and we didn't like fighting so much in trying to do so much. If these things were the "good things in life" and we were supposed to be having a "GOOD TIME", then why didn't we feel good?

We didn't travel often while we were raising our family, had a limited income, and were concentrating on building a place for ourselves in our professions. When we were ready to travel again after eighteen years, it was Perry who initiated our plans. He wanted to try out *his* way of travel for us, much like a warrior coming to reclaim his rights from his wife's family's domination. Perry wanted us to celebrate his success and accomplishments in business with grand travels to foreign places, but what I wanted and needed most was to rent a small housekeeping cottage where I could cook, walk, draw, and write during my summers off from teaching. During the school year I often traveled to various parts of the country to train teachers, and summers seemed the time to stay in one place. Since we didn't want to fight and Perry clearly wanted his way for us, I needed to learn the art of compromising my short-term needs in favor of my long-term goal, which was to enhance our marriage by forming an indomitable team in which neither of us lost our identities.

As we went Perry's way (and it wasn't easy for me to do that!), I began to set limits on the amount I could see and do, and he began to see the value in each moment. We were having a better time. Gradually, he incorporated what *I* needed and wanted into *his* plans so that *we* were able to move to our primary purpose in traveling—to satisfy both ourselves and one another rather than anyone else.

Of course, none of the stages we had gone through in developing our purpose for travel was absolutely pure in being "my way," "his way," or "our way." "Our way" trips now still include times when Perry needs, wants, or insists on having his way and I need, want, or insist on having mine. The success of each trip depends a great deal on the strength of each of our needs and desires, sense of humor, and willingness to compromise for the satisfaction of both.

Travelers can go through one or more of these stages at various times on their voyages or in their lives at home. Some progress from one stage to another and then go back and forth in varying degrees as we have done, some remain content in one of the stages throughout their lives, some stay in one stage for a longer time than others, while still other travelers move in and out of all the stages in one trip. There is no "right" or "wrong" stage. What is important is to recognize the stage you are in and try to understand the reasons you are or aren't getting along. Then you can choose to continue your patterns or to change them to your individual and joint needs.

For example, take Jack and Laura. Jack likes to plan trips *his* way because he has know-how and wants to teach Laura what he loves in travel. Laura is happy to go Jack's way because she wants to learn and share with her partner what he has to offer. For this couple, going "his" way is satisfying for both. However, in other couples, each partner may want his or her own way; some couples need and enjoy conflict whereas others do not. Donald and Kate enjoy arguing and disputing; they find that their fighting is constructive. But other couples argue because they don't know of alternatives; although their fighting is destructive, they are more comfortable fighting than they would be learning not to fight. But couples who are willing can discover ways to meet their separate needs and learn techniques to make satisfying compromises (see Chapter 2).

Why do you travel?

Do you and your partner want to travel for the same or different reasons?

Do you argue more than you'd like to?

What are our specific reasons for traveling nowadays? Perry travels because:

> I'm curious. I want to see what's on the other side of the street. It might enhance my life. I like my creative and artistic way of planning. I like the challenge of finding comfort away from home while exploring beautiful places away from crowds. I can make up for feeling deprived when I was young by celebrating what I have earned now. I travel some to satisfy my desire for status, some to restore myself, and I want to celebrate with Margot.

And now I know why I want to travel: to celebrate my relationship with Perry as well as my accomplishments with my family and profession. I love to study our interactions and discover similarities and differences between us and other people. I like to feel I am an actress in the world's theater and also a member of the audience responding to an everyday performance. I like to feel alive in all my senses, and to gain perspective. Most of all, I like to know that I am helping Perry to do what he wants most, which is to travel. With the delight and fulfillment he gains from our travels together he is most willing to encourage me in what I want to do in my personal and professional life at home.

You might enjoy writing down your reasons for traveling, as it may help you to focus on your activities before you reach your destination. It might help to think of a specific trip, either your last trip or the next one you would like to take.

ARE YOU READY TO TRAVEL?

Are you ready to leave home? I always used to have an immediate and unvarying answer to that question: "Of course I'm ready! Isn't everybody always ready to travel? Let's just go." Why did I answer with such a quick-firing yes? I liked thinking of myself as a good sport, always ready to escape or seek glamorous adventures. Isn't everyone supposed to be like that? If I had said, "No, I'm not ready," I would've been thought crazy, as if refusing a diamond or a gold bar. Even though I had sinking feelings and doubts, I pushed them aside, as if I could banish them.

Sometimes worries would float back up, "But what about?" and "But what if?" I rarely let myself finish those questions. Yet the swarm of unarticulated doubts and fears followed me on vacation; my persistent uneasiness prevented me from enjoying myself and from knowing why I couldn't enjoy myself. When I did try to name my fears they tumbled out: What would happen without me at home? Would I still have a place? Would someone take over what I did at work? Would he or she do better than I? If so, what would become of me?

Gradually, I realized that if I am afraid I'll lose my place while I'm away then I'm not ready to enjoy my travels and I'll be a drag on any trip. Before I go I need to recognize that some fears are unfounded and to prepare myself to deal with those that seem real.

Are you prepared for the unexpected when you are away? Even if you have carefully planned, you can't plan for everything. All sorts of situations arise that require you to cope with the unexpected: moving from one locale to another, searching for hotels, plane delays, driving long stretches without seeing a gas station, trying to order food from a menu written in a language you don't know. Try to plan your trips to take your particular anxieties into account. For example, we stay in one locale for at least four or five nights and take a variety of day trips so that we don't have to move from place to place too often.

There are times, however, when we somehow fall into a trap of thinking that because we have planned so carefully we are protected from anything that would make us anxious. The worst is when I'm so inflexible that I don't expect the unexpected, and when it comes I am taken by unpleasant surprise. First I become indignant and outraged: "How could this happen to me when I planned so carefully?" Then I blame myself: "I didn't plan carefully enough"; or I blame the world for having betrayed me: "After I've worked so hard I deserve better than this." But the truth is that there is no guarantee that life will go exactly as planned. What happens is what happens, and the best we can do is to take it as an experience from which to learn and make the best of it.

Knowing how much change you are ready for can help you decide how many places to go and how long to stay in each. Some "Expedition Seekers" thrive on change and repeatedly search for new adventures. If you are very adaptable to change you will be less anxious than those of us who are more resistant to sharp or frequent deviations. You can visit more places if you choose to, and remain in good humor with a sense of well-being.

"Homing Pigeons" don't relish leaving the familiar good life at home to face unpredictable challenges abroad. Satisfied "Fat Cats" don't like to travel often, preferring to rest at home savoring their last set of adventures before going away again. "Swallows to Capistrano" may decide to return to a favorite place each year, taking one or two new day trips. Such return visits allow them to slowly blend unfamiliar and familiar experiences. "Model Martyrs" don't really want to travel but do so with an attitude of self-sacrifice.

If you are wary of change, each move to a new place or each new activity can mean more discomfort, which can lead to poor humor and more fights. I know how grouchy and mean I become when I try to cram in more than feels comfortable. Sometimes I envy "Flexible Flyers" who take what comes in their stride with what appears to be so much ease. But I enjoy what I do, see, hear, feel, and touch in great detail, and the quality of each experience matters more to me than the number of times I travel, or the number of places I visit.

Are you prepared for changes that will take place at home while you're away? I like to know what I'm coming back to before I leave. I spend a good deal of time, energy, and caring to build strong family, friend, and work relationships. The strength of these ties usually helps me to travel with a sense of well-being. But at times I've returned to find that people close to me have made changes that I didn't anticipate. I'm talking here about relatively minor changes—not serious illness or death—but if you don't allow for such changes, you may be disappointed when you return.

Much as we may like to think we are indispensable, we are not. We may be impossible to replace exactly, and very valuable in making decisions at home and at work, but life does go on without us, sometimes for the worse, and sometimes for the better. For instance, in your absence your boss might assign you a new job or arrange for you to work side by side with someone you don't like. Or, while you are away your child might do better at school than when you're home. You need to consider whether these are reasons to prevent you from going on your trip or to stop you from having the enjoyable time you have earned.

Change is part of the travel package, change during the trip, and upon your return. If you can acknowledge your skills and resources to handle change, then you are really ready to leave home.

Write down what you expect to stay the same when you return and what you expect to change.

After thinking or writing, you might enjoy, as we have, playing a game to see how close your expectation comes to what actually happens rather than focusing on worrying about something you can't do anything about.

How do you know you are ready to leave? Perry and I are usually ready to travel when we recognize how much we have earned a treat after working hard throughout the year. By "work" we mean putting our effort into both our personal and professional relationships and accomplishments. When we feel ready to leave home we ask ourselves, "Have we earned our way to treating ourselves to a trip, and will we be able to treat ourselves to as much pleasure as possible in view of the difficulties of travel?"

> Traveling is a brutality. It forces you to trust strangers and to lose sight of all that familiar comfort of home and friends. You are constantly off balance. Nothing is yours except the essential things—air, sleep, dreams, the sun, the sky—all things tending toward the eternal or what we imagine of it.[2]

2. Ceasare Pavese, cited by Ian McEwan in *The Comfort of Strangers* (New York: Washington Square Press, 1981), preface.

The traveler's paradox is how to feel at home while being away. Perry and I are ready to go when we have accepted the challenge of finding ways to make ourselves as comfortable as possible while exploring strange and new territory.

Are you ready to take on the challenge of making yourself as comfortable as possible?

If not, what is your particular challenge?

ARE YOU FINANCIALLY READY TO TRAVEL?

How much can you afford to spend on travel or vacation? Most financial experts advise limiting the cost of a vacation to between 3 percent and 6 percent of your annual income. If travel is high on your list of priorities and you want to take an expensive vacation, you might consider giving up something else in order to afford the trip. But it usually doesn't pay to go on a trip if you have to suffer financially and emotionally for the rest of the year.

Look at your budget and see if you can make a trade-off after making a list of your potential gains and losses in taking an expensive vacation; for if you'd like a new car and can't afford both the car and a trip to Europe, you might choose the new car and decide to take your vacation stateside. Or, you might decide you really needed to get away, that you would gain more perspective or new skills by taking the trip, and you can delay buying a new car. Would you settle for a used one? Or would you use charge cards for your trip?

If you give up taking a vacation because of limited funds, what will you lose as far as your attitude at work is concerned? If your morale is low will that affect your production so that you end up losing more than you gain in personal and professional satisfaction? How difficult it is to decide where to put your money?

What are your priorities?

Do you feel comfortable or uncomfortable with the amount you spend on travel or vacations now?

If you spent more or less what would you gain or lose?

Do you want to make a change or keep your spending about the same?

ARE YOU READY TO TAKE TIME FOR TRAVEL?

When to take a vacation and how long you can be away from your job or profession depends on your work situation and how comfortable you are about being away.

Unemployed. If you are unemployed at the present time because of being laid off, fired, between school and career, between jobs, or looking for a new profession you might ask yourself:

How long do I feel comfortable being away without employment or away from home?

How ambitious am I in finding work (paid or unpaid), establishing or reestablishing a career?

Self-Employed. If you are self-employed (within or outside of an organization), or are an artist, philanthropist, housewife, househusband, or retired person, you might need to consider how much work you can delegate to others, how competent your assistants are, and if it is feasible or appealing to combine business and pleasure on one trip. If you feel vaguely uncomfortable about leaving and can't put your finger on why, you might ask yourself these questions:

Would I feel more relaxed if I could do some business by phone or letter while I am away?

How long can I be unavailable to clients, customers, or patients, or ask them to use substitutes without my worrying too much or their needs suffering?

Am I worried about how much work might pile up while I am away?

Do I have enough energy, organizational skills, and ability to handle accumulated work or personnel problems?

Employee. If you are employed by someone else, you need to find out how long your boss or the system will allow you to be away. If you feel somewhat anxious about traveling and are not sure why, you might ask yourself:

What would I gain or lose if I took a vacation at this time?

How confident or threatened do I feel in my position?

Will time off for travel be held against me or prevent me from advancing as quickly as I would like?

How much resentment or jealousy can I accept from an employee or fellow employees who aren't taking a vacation?

What deadlines do I have to meet before I leave and when I return?

How many changes can I adjust to if changes are likely in my absence?

CAN YOU COMBINE A BUSINESS AND PLEASURE TRIP?

Some people rarely take a vacation—they say they wouldn't know what to do with one—but are willing to travel for business, which is often their pleasure. In this group are people who love their work and can pace themselves so well between work and leisure time throughout the year that they don't feel a need for a vacation; others are workaholics.

Yet other travelers endure business trips because they are mandatory; however, they combine them with a few days or a few weeks of vacation. Such vacations are often convenient and affordable because almost all of the trip is paid for by the business or professional organization. At conventions one may need only put in a token appearance, but other trips are strictly business and leave very little time for leisure.

Some trips are planned to honor or reward business people, professionals in various fields, or volunteers for the fine quality of their work. While some people enjoy these honorary trips as a celebration of their success and an opportunity for public recognition of their achievement, others find them more exhausting than working at home. Some honorees feel they lose more than they gain because they lose business at home while they are away. Trips that require meeting and greeting people all day long can end up being more of a punishment than a reward. The company may even send the honorees to a place where they don't want to be—to an overcrowded, hot city halfway around the world. Then an honoree's only solace may be to remark, "Well, at least I can say I've been there and I never have to go back!" Even trips to restful vacation spots such as Hawaii or the Caribbean can turn into difficult times if the focus is on meeting and being with people when you are tired and need a well-earned rest. The price of recognition of accomplishments is sometimes not worth the exhaustion, and loss of pleasure.

A spouse or friend sometimes accompanies a partner on business trips. For a spouse, a business trip can be a blissful respite, an exciting adventure, a glittery status symbol, or a sentence of solitary confinement. Before departure, partners can discuss one another's needs and expectations. For example, if one partner is going primarily to support the other or to fulfill social obligations, his or her partner might offer to do something as a gift of equal value to minimize the tag-along partner's resentment on the trip. Explore activities that will genuinely interest the spouse who will not be in the business goings-on. Can he or she use the opportunity of the trip to pursue independent interests?

Women accompanying their husbands or men friends often feel a special trepidation about venturing outside their hotel unescorted. If you find yourself in this predicament, begin by reading books or brochures in your hotel room, paying attention to anything that catches your eye. Museums and churches are usually safe places to visit alone, and guided sightseeing tours provide safety and company. Take a sightseeing bus tour to discover what the city or town has to offer. You can return to various spots as you feel more confident. If you venture forth slowly, doing just one thing at a time, you may find you enjoy your solo adventures during your partner's business hours.

If you are going on a business trip combined with pleasure ask yourself some of these questions:

Is going on a business trip a way to save money?

Can you combine the trip with pleasure?

What will you gain from taking the pleasure part of the trip in this way? What will you lose?

If you are accompanying someone on a trip what parts do you expect to enjoy? What parts make you uncomfortable?

What independent interests do you want to pursue?

If you want to wait in the hotel room for your mate, what will you and your mate gain and lose?

If your purpose for going on the trip is to help your mate, what would you like to receive in return for your support?

Do you really dislike travel and don't want to admit it either to yourself or your partner?

If you admitted to your secret what is the worst thing that might happen? What is the best?

Is admitting it to your partner worth the risk?

ARE YOU READY TO LEAVE YOUR FAMILY?

Leaving a family can bring out particular apprehensions. Questions arise: "How will children get home when the baby sitter's car breaks down?" "Who will drive my mother to the doctor?" "Do I trust Alison to care for my family?"

If you find a person you can trust to care for your children or parents you have a better chance of returning with a new perspective that will enable you to better handle problems at home. However, if you leave your family with an unreliable or inadequate care-taker, you run the risk of coming back to find problems even worse than when you left, so that the vacation turns out to be more of a burden than a success.

When children or parents thrive while you're away, if you are one of the "The Pridefuls" you can share your pleasure in their accomplishments and celebrate their resourcefulness and independence; and can pat yourself on the back for having helped them to acquire the skills they need.

However, if you are one of the "Need-to-be-Needed-ers" you'll be tempted to put yourself down for not having done a good enough job: "I'm not needed after all. (Poor me!)" But this position is a trap that spoils your own and your family's delight in their ability to take care while you're away.

What can you take pride in when you leave your family?

What are your concerns?

If you are not satisfied with the care-taking arrangements now can you make any changes? If so, what kind?

If not, does the situation at home make you too apprehensive to leave? Do you need to stay home for your own peace of mind?

If you do stay home will you resent it? What will you gain and lose by staying home?

ARE YOU PHYSICALLY READY TO TRAVEL?

Deciding where to go and how to travel will depend, in part, on your physical well-being and limitations. Some considerations are:

- Do you have special dietary or medical needs? Should you plan to take along specific food and medicines from home?
- Do you need to be near medical facilities?
- Do you have the stamina to walk or hike? Have you prepared for physical activity on the trip by practicing before you go?
- Are you able to be comfortable in a car, plane, or bus for long periods of time?
- Do you have adequate health insurance?
- Do you need special pillows, blankets, heating pads, or other devices?
- What do you do in case of emergencies?

If you have physical limitations or medical problems and are traveling outside of the United States, you can find out what facilities are available, as well as names of English-speaking doctors by contacting the International Association for Medical Assistance to Travelers (IAMAT, 736 Center St. Lewiston, New York, 14092) for a free directory of doctors and medical centers in 125 countries and territories. Doctors who belong to this association agree to a set payment schedule for members ($20 for office visits, $25 for house or hotel visits). Travelers are advised to write for information six to eight weeks before leaving for overseas.

You can also contact the U.S. Department of Health to find out what inoculations you might need and how much time you must allow for a series of injections and for any side effects. You can phone or write U.S. embassies or consulate services, information bureaus, and travel agencies. You can call ahead to Chambers of Commerce, hotels, and inns to inform them of your problems and to ask questions so you can be assured as much as possible that you will have your needs cared for.

If you have a particular disability and need a wheelchair, phone airlines and hotels in advance to find out how they can accommodate you. If you need a stretcher, the airline needs 72 hours' notice, and you will need to purchase three seats! If you have a chronic condition such as heart ailment or diabetes, contact your local heart or diabetic association for special information. Many hotels, restaurants, and airlines cater to people with special dietary needs, but you cannot always count on getting food at the exact time you need it. And places that advertise salt-free and diabetic foods do not keep their promises. For reassurance, carry special foods with you from home.

You can call your doctor at home to be sure you have enough of your prescription drugs, as well as any other drug you might need in the event diarrhea or insomnia strikes, or if you venture into unaccustomed territory in particularly high altitudes. You can also ask for prescriptions to be refilled on the trip. If you contact your health insurance company before you leave you can find out whom to contact away from home, if you can use your insurance forms while on the trip, or, if not, what information you will need for your insurance company when you return home. Before you leave, be sure you have your health identification card, medical bracelet (if needed), and at least a three days' supply of vitamins and medications in your carry-on luggage in case you and your checked baggage part company. You can allay many fears if you are prepared to cope with your medical needs.

Even if you are physically fit or have planned carefully to take care of your special problems, emergencies arise. It is difficult to trust new medical people and strange hospitals. However, even at home you will sometimes receive sensitive and excellent care but other times get the run-around through red tape and inefficient bureaucracies. In an emergency, one question that might help you to make a decision is: "What are advantages and disadvantages of staying where I am (for an operation on a broken limb, for example) or going home?"

"Worry-Warts" imagine they might get sick and die away from home. Many fears stem from fantasies that they will be left alone, uncared for, not knowing whom to contact. Though emergencies do happen, they are rare, and assistance is almost always available. You can protect yourself financially by taking out a special "trip interruption insurance" policy before you leave home. Phone your insurance company for details, then decide if you want to pay the price of the policy or take your chances.

There are, of course, minor crises that survivors enjoy retelling, though they were miserable at the time. For instance, on the morning of departure, Chester and Louise were in the Orly Airport, Paris, with her relatives. Louise was green—not only green—but vomiting, with accompanying attacks of diarrhea. She was sure her relatives had poisoned her with old seafood; however, she didn't want to hurt their feelings by accusing them of doing her in. She just prayed for time to pass and for no one to look at her when she went in and out of the restroom. Each moment she said to herself, "If I just get through this minute," and the next, and so on.

Chester hardly dared look at her because whenever he did he said to himself, "Please, Louise, not here! Don't die here!" At the boarding gate Louise could barely muster a polite smile of goodbye to her cousins. Chester waved vigorously, as if to cover for both of them. When they made it onto the plane and sat down, Louise grabbed four airsick bags and lay them on her lap. Chester helped to settle her, avoiding the look on her green face, repeating to himself, "Louise, you've gotta make it! We're going HOME." Out of nervousness he struck up a conservation with a man sitting next to him to take his mind off Louise. As the plane took off he began to breathe more deeply and realize there was *help* available on that plane. He was not alone, and that made all the difference in the world. The flight attendant *did* have dramamine. Louise's sickness passed and they made it without further incident, and both agreed the best part was living to tell the tale!

What are your physical limitations?

What do you have to consider in planning to take care of your limitations?

What do you think you will do in cases of emergency?

WHAT ARE YOUR INTERESTS OR HOBBIES?

Many travelers have so many fascinations that their problem is to limit their activities so they don't end up like children at a birthday party who gorge themselves on too much cake and ice cream.

"History Buffs" can hardly wait to visit the sights that have intrigued their curiosity for so long. They enjoy visiting ancient ruins, stumbling occasionally upon shards of past civilizations, as if looking for a part of themselves. "Exotica-Seekers" relish being the envy of their friends as they take elite adventures: trekking over mountains in Tibet, photographing rhinoceri on African safaris, or even taking the Siberian railroad for Christmas. "Palace Researchers" find glamor in imagining what their lives would be like in a world of royalty. "Social Reformers" visit poorer countries to study human conditions or perhaps to say, "There but for the grace of God go I." "Curious Conversationalists" like to chat with local townspeople or want to practice speaking foreign languages.

Artists, writers, musicians, and students explore special haunts to develop their talents and hone their skills. Birdwatchers and flower-lovers flock to the meadows, and wine and food-tasters gather in favorite bistros, cafés, castles, and caves.

But you don't have to know your interests before traveling. You can develop them along the way. Something might catch your eye as you drive along a country road, walk down a side street in a town, or stand in the middle of a city square. For instance, I never knew how much I like street markets until I walked in one. The sights and smells of cheeses, fish, olives, sausages, and displays of herbs, with people of all ages buying and selling, intrigued me so much that we began to plan day trips to include a street market whenever we could.

Though there is delight in discovering and developing interests as you travel, if you don't have any notions before leaving home, you run the risk of feeling that you are being carted around, doing what you dislike. Many travelers happen upon interests by trial-and-error, but if you have a limited amount of time to experiment, particularly on an expensive vacation, you may want to carefully consider your interests so you won't be disappointed. Don't worry about what you "should" see—just begin to think about what you like to do at home. If you are a business person you might want to visit a similar type of business in another town or city. If you like window-shopping at home, you might enjoy window-shopping abroad. Beginning with familiar interests will help you to feel less tentative away from home and may even lead you to discover new interests.

"Nothing happens to me in a city that isn't useful," Jan Morris says. "People always want to be helpful and suggest things for me to do, but they don't realize that buying some paper in a drugstore is just as valuable to me as meeting Mayor Koch."[3]

Just strolling or sitting in foreign cafes and parks can be quite fascinating. Simply pretend that you are the audience for a theatrical event—all the world's a stage. You may find yourself intrigued by observing how people conduct their daily lives in different parts of the world.

Enjoy the diversity, if you can. Try to appreciate differences without judging them as better or worse than American conventions and styles.

What are your interests at home?

How can you pursue those interests on your trip?

What new activities are suggested by the places you'd like to visit?

Would you like to discover your interests through trial-and-error as you travel?

If you are a sports enthusiast you may choose to focus on your particular sport or activity for all or part of your vacation. Golf, tennis, fishing, sailing, bicycling, backpacking for long-distance hikes,

3. David Roberts, "A Traveler's Eye," interview with Jan Morris, *Geo Magazine*, October 1984, p. 56.

or short-distance walks or rambles can be planned as close to home or as far away as you like. Part of your considerations depend on: the amount of time and money you have; your age, experience, and degree of energy (or lack of it); dietary and physical limitations; and where you want to go.

If you like to sail and have limited amounts of money and time, you could rent a boat or crew on a friend's motorcraft. You might want to join with others to share rental expenses. If you have a larger vacation budget you might go on a cruise.

Rambling is a special kind of recreational activity that I will describe in detail in Chapter 4 because Perry and I have chosen it as our favorite kind of "sports" activity; and you might also delight in it.

Do you want to focus on a particular sport or recreational activity for all or part of your vacation? If so, which sport or activity?

What do you have to consider in order to take this kind of vacation?

WHERE TO TRAVEL?

A yearning to travel is the beginning of fulfilling a dream. Some travelers want only to go, without caring about the where.

> For my part, I travel not to go anywhere but to go. I travel for travel's sake, the great affair is to move.[4]

Other travelers care very much about where they go. Some of you may have since childhood dreamt about visiting a mountain you had read about or seen a picture of. You may have heard from a relative, teacher, or friend who enthusiastically described a work of art in a particularly beautiful place. An idea of where to go can come to you any time or place: walking down a street, sitting in a restaurant, staring into space, talking with a friend as you reminisce over past vacations; or reading a travel brochure or magazine article.

4. Robert Louis Stevenson, *Travels with a Donkey.*

Where you go and how many places you visit depend on:

- your interests
- the amount of energy, money, and time you have
- the kind of travel you like
- how much travel experience you have had
- your skill in speaking a foreign language or your degree of comfort even if you don't understand the language
- your desire to gain an overall picture of a region or country or to focus on a specific area
- the amount of change you enjoy or can tolerate without losing your sense of pleasure
- your preference for collecting many experiences or savoring a few.

Spend some time thinking about each of these topics. Weigh the advantages and disadvantages of the alternatives.

For example, if you haven't traveled a lot or if you feel that you will have only one chance in a lifetime to travel to a special region or country, you may want to try to visit as many towns and sights as you can in the time available. Your overview trip would give you an opportunity to survey a variety of places. But if your survey is too broad or too fast paced, you may forget much of what you see and lose your good humor. The more you try to do and see the more decisions you'll have to make and the more chances for transportation delays and foul-ups.

If instead you decide to focus on a specific area and savor a few experiences, you'll have the time to really appreciate and learn from your adventures. But you may feel disappointed about what you have missed by not seeing and doing more. Travelers who choose a limited itinerary should do so believing that their glass is half full rather than half empty—or perhaps completely filled by the sense of well-being that comes from going to the exact place they want to go and seeing and doing precisely as much as they are ready for.

A dialogue written by Sada Murayama portrays an internal debate on this topic.

(Scene: Balcony of a hotel room overlooking St. Peter's)

Doer: Well, so here you are—another wonderful autumn day in Rome, languishing over the railing of your balcony sipping your third cup of coffee. There are places to see, sounds to hear—and you're reading a book!

Contemplater: What's the hurry? What have you to see and hear *with*? I wish to catch the essence, the significance of the world about me.
Doer: From a book?
Contemplater: For information, yes. The rest is up to the individual. It's more important to *feel* what you've seen than the number of places or things.
Doer: But time is slipping by—you have only two days left.
Contemplater: Do not frighten me with lack of time. I'd rather really *see* a corner of the Sistine Chapel than join the group rushing through.
Doer: You will be sorry when you get back. What can you tell your friends?
Contemplater: But I am telling myself. Isn't that more important?[5]

Where would you like to go?

Do you have the time, energy, and money to go where you would like?

If not, what would you be willing to give up or trade off?

Would you prefer to survey a region or country or to focus on a specific area? What are the advantages and disadvantages of each?

HOW DO YOU CHOOSE A TRAVEL PARTNER?

If you already have a partner, of course you already know who will accompany you on your travels, unless you choose to take separate vacations.

If you are single and want to travel with another person there are qualities you might look for. A woman who has traveled a great deal with her husband, a variety of friends, as well as one or two family members, told us her criteria:

> I want to travel with a person who doesn't fret about home all the time. My companion needs to share some of my interests,

5. My thanks to Sada for permission to print her dialogue.

> though not all of them—but I'd like him or her to have awareness, curiosity, a sense of discovery, and to respect my enthusiasms even if they are not the same as my partner's.
>
> I'd like my partner to share with me what he or she is seeing and feeling. I'd like us to share our interests in other people, and enjoy food and drink as part of the pleasure of being together.
>
> My partner must have enough stamina to keep going with the changes that occur in travel, and respect my limitations. I don't want my partner to do more driving in the car than I feel comfortable with. If my partner goes faster than I do (walks faster, or takes in more sights than I) I don't want to be pulled around. I want my partner to tell me that he or she needs to be on the move for longer periods of time, or go faster so I can decide whether I want to go along or find something for myself to do alone. I want my partner to be independent enough to do things alone when he or she wants or needs to, as long as it isn't a mischievous deed that would hurt me.
>
> I don't want to hear many complaints, especially about my companion's health. I don't want my partner to be too involved with the quality of accommodations or to complain about the place we're staying if something goes wrong.

A less-experienced traveler added:

> I want to travel with a person who likes to talk about personal values and people's motivations and personalities. I like to go on a trip with a person who is willing to make mistakes and allow me to make them without putting either of us down. I really need to feel I can be spontaneous, not plotting and planning all the time.

Marilyn Bender writes that she would cast her vote for a child as an ideal companion:

> For an adventurous and possibly difficult trip, what better than someone too old to require a baby sitter but too young to vote? Someone with a strong back and a curious mind, recently acquainted with the language of the country.[6]

6. Marilyn Bender, "Two For the Road," *New York Times*, Travel Section, Sunday, December 4, 1984, p. 45.

Jens Jurgen, director of Travel Companion Exchange (Post Office Box 833, Amityville, New York 11701), runs a service for travelers seeking compatible partners. The organization's more than 2,000 members pay $48.00 a year to receive monthly listings. Some of the questions Mr. Jurgen suggests asking to determine the compatibility of a prospective traveling companion are:

- Can you accept cockroaches and primitive plumbing or do you need perfectly clean rooms?
- Do you take in the town in one day or do you prefer to digest a few attractions on each visit?
- Are you an early arriver at airports, or a cliff-hanger, arriving at the last minute?
- Are you a spendthrift, or an economizer?
- How tolerant are you if your partner gets sick?
- Are you willing to have your partner be free to accept engagements without you?
- Do you want separate rooms?

Knowing what qualities you want in a partner can help you in planning, making compromises, and setting realistic expectations so that your trip is more enjoyable. In addition, qualities you like in a partner when you travel may also be qualities you would like in your travels through life at home with a partner.

What are your criteria for a traveling companion? (What qualities do you like)?

Which of your partner's criteria are the same as yours?

Which are different?

WHAT DO YOU EXPECT OF YOURSELF AS A TRAVELER?

Some travelers expect to be "ideal" tourists: content with whatever comes their way, always relaxed and in good humor, enjoying everything and having a wonderful time—with nary a problem, worry, or complaint. Somehow, "ideal" travelers believe that on a trip they will magically enjoy activities that they detest at home. I am thinking about a man I saw standing in an art museum, first on one foot, then the other, mopping his brow, sighing. "I just hate museums," he said, "and at home I never set foot in them. But I thought I should do it at least when I travel. That's what you're supposed to do, isn't it?"

And some couples expect their relationship to be perfect on a trip: no fighting, no differences in opinions. But heat, crowds, foreign foods and languages, exhaustion, delays, or getting lost can try even the best of relationships. Fortunately, you can avoid some squabbling and disappointment by discussing and planning for each of your individual needs. And you can avoid some disillusionment by expecting that you won't be ideal travelers in an ideal relationship.

First time travelers, especially, need to be wary of trusting travel brochures that suggest that all they need to do to have a good time is relax because they will be taken care of. If you book a package tour, your transportation, sightseeing, and accommodations will be arranged for you. However, no tour can help you cope with unexpected or unpleasant situations—plane delays, rough weather, or strange surroundings. Odd as it may sound at first, to have a good vacation you'll need to work at it. Your vacation is a well-earned treat, but you can't expect a travel agent to handle everything.

A young woman reported, "I really learned something when we went on vacation and I didn't want to bring myself (the person I am at home) on the trip. I just wanted things to work out, to be taken care of away from home. I was so disappointed because I thought everything would be ideal. We didn't even think about what made us comfortable or uncomfortable with ourselves in new surroundings."

One of the dangers in setting your expectations too high, beyond who you are and what you are able to do, is that you will be disappointed, frustrated, or angry at a time you had wanted to be special. Few of us are always as good as we want to be or think we *should* be. Lost on a road in a foreign country, we tell ourselves that we *should* be alert enough not to lose our way at all, or we *should* at least take mishaps in stride. But perhaps the best thing to do is double-check the map and chant a chorus of "This too will pass." It's important, I think, not to always expect yourself to be perfect, nor to lose empathy and perspective by demanding more of yourself and the trip than makes sense. High standards are fine, as long as you don't expect yourself to be the "ideal" traveler or to be different from who you are.

Realistic expectations enable most travelers to become acclimated more quickly, feel less anxious, and have more fun. Also hotel employees, shopkeepers, and local residents tend to be more patient and generous to travelers who present themselves as newcomers or novices rather than pretending to be more knowledgeable or sophisticated than they really are.

Though feeling somewhat awkward and shy is uncomfortable, you may find that preferable to the pressure of trying to appear as though you know what you're doing when you don't. How can you know something before you've experienced it? What's the point in trying to fool strangers? If you accept your naiveté and show the curiosity, sense of wonder, and excitement that children have, you might more fully appreciate the strangeness of a new situation.

"I think it's an aspect of innocence," says Jan Morris. "I'm truly guileless. And that opens doors. You learn more if you're absolutely frank and tell people you don't understand something."[7]

You might even want to set your expectations of yourself somewhat lower than how you really think you will act on the trip. If you then do better than you expected, you'll have cause for celebration. For instance, if you know that you get anxious, upset, or angry if you get lost on a highway, allow yourself a few mistakes each day, and cheer if you don't reach your limit.

So, rather than denigrate yourself for having needs, idiosyncrasies, and personal tics, think of ways to satisfy them. Trying to be the "ideal" traveler is too burdensome a chore to assign yourself on your vacation.

How might you fall into the trap of being the "ideal" traveler?

What expectations of yourself do you have that might be too high or unrealistic?

How will you feel if your trip does not match all your expectations?

What are some realistic expectations of yourself as a traveler?

How will you feel if you exceed your expectations on the trip?

7. David Roberts, "A Traveler's Eye," interview with Jan Morris, *Geo Magazine*, October 1984, p. 56.

HOW DO YOU KNOW IF YOU'VE HAD A SUCCESSFUL VACATION?

Each traveler has his or her own way of judging if a vacation has been successful. Here is a random sampling:

- Having a good time.
- Learning something valuable, even from an unpleasant experience.
- Eating delicious food and sampling wines.
- Satisfying personal interests (strolling, studying in a museum or library, or shopping).
- Not fighting with one another.
- Fighting constructively with one another.
- Taking a break from discussing interpersonal problems.
- Making progress on a difficult problem.

In short, some travelers' criteria for success are based primarily on the tangible products of their travels (such as gifts or photographs of sights), while others' are based on the process (such as how they communicate with their partners).

What does having a "good time" mean to you?

If you know what makes a successful vacation for you, you may be better prepared to plan your trip. You will also be able to identify which aspects contributed to your success. Sometimes it helps to first think of how you felt after taking a vacation that failed for you. What helped that trip to fail? If you know how you don't want to feel, you're on your way to discovering success.

Think about a vacation that wasn't successful for you:

What happened that made you feel it was a failure? (For example, you felt exhausted, disliked your partner more than when you left, were disappointed at not seeing and doing more, overate).

What actions could you take to prevent a recurrence? (For example, lower expectations, better planning, less hectic itinerary, more careful budgeting).

Perry knows he has had a successful vacation when he comes back feeling inspired, refreshed, relaxed, excited about our relationship and wanting to continue to work on it and celebrate it, able to laugh with himself and me. He knows the vacation has been an especially good one when he thinks of a new idea that will make his life better at home or at work.

I know I've had a successful vacation when I come back with energy to paint, draw, write, and work. We are both pleased when we've comforted one another and come up with alternatives to fighting. We are triumphant when we've spent long hours feeling comfortable with each other, when we've done something delightfully spontaneous, and when we know we can apply what we've learned to our lives at home.

We also know the vacation has been successful when circumstances have cooperated. For example, the plane departed almost on schedule and did not develop motor trouble in the air, our hotel reservations were honored with quiet rooms, the places we visited were beautiful, the weather was not too hot, and the customs officials were efficient.

How would you expect to feel after a successful vacation?

What would you and your partner need to have done for you to call your vacation successful?

2

Joint Planning: The Art of Compromise

You have decided to travel with a partner. Now the two of you might want to plan your trip so that you will each find it successful. The planning will have to take into account your individual purposes, desires, needs, and expectations. On some issues you'll agree, on others you won't; this chapter focuses on the latter issues and suggests ways to develop your own special plan.

The primary strategy is to discover and explore potential disagreements *before* you leave home. You'll both then have an opportunity to think about creative alternatives to fighting, harboring grudges, pouting, and destructive uses of anger. If you determine the budget for the trip and who pays for what before you go, you won't find yourselves arguing on a London street corner. If you now make compromises about how much baggage you will take, you can avoid quarrels at the Vienna train station. And if certain special problems remain unresolved before your departure, you'll at least know when and where to expect disagreements.

To discover basic issues on which you agree or disagree, you and your partner might like to compare your responses to some of the topics discussed in Chapter 1:

- Your reasons for travel
- Your readiness to depart; how much change you expect
- Your physical, psychological, and financial limitations
- Your professional and family obligations
- Your interests
- Where you want to go

- **Your expectations of one another away from home**
- **Your criteria for a successful vacation**

AREAS OF AGREEMENT

It is usually easiest to begin your planning by considering the areas in which you agree. Here's a partial list of things that Perry and I agree on:

One of our major purposes in travel is to restore and replenish ourselves both mentally and physically. We like to visit small, quiet, beautiful places: gardens, towns, the seaside, and moors. We also like good, small hotels and restaurants that serve a variety of fine food and wines.

We have both learned that we stay in better humor if we limit our activities and move at a slow pace. When driving we like to stop quite often for food, drinks, or visits to churches, museums, and shops. We occasionally like going to a large town or city for a day or so, and every other trip to a city for five to seven days.

We are both interested in beautiful architecture and art (particularly primitive work and medieval gargoyles). We both like to read about the history of a place before or after visiting it, but never during the actual visit. We like to walk three to six miles a day, admire wildflowers, wander in local streets and shops, read novels and tour books, and write in our journals. We enjoy drawing and painting together (pencil, charcoal, and watercolor). Perry usually draws buildings or landscapes, while I paint landscapes and make humorous line-drawing sketches of travelers or local people.

We also love to have long rests, to take unhurried baths and showers, to gossip, to take strolls after dinner, and go to bed early. We like talking about our careers, about what we appreciate and resent about our times together, and about our family—to talk leisurely in a way that we don't have enough time for at home.

We both hate jet lag, long drives, heat, waiting in lines, tour buses, crowds, business, and we refuse steadfastly to hear lectures about what we are seeing. We have a particular prejudice against places that try to be something they are not, or more than what they are.

Our biases, however, are ours. We even like them, recognizing them as part of our personalities and values. We know, too, that our pet distastes are often other travelers' delights. For instance, some very good friends of ours love guided tours so much that they discreetly sneak up behind a tour group to eavesdrop.

Preferences are subjective: there are not "right" or "wrong" things to like or dislike. Just respect your own ways and tastes. After all, this is your vacation, your celebrations, your trip for no one but you. We hope that you stand up for your values if they are different from those of your relatives, colleagues, and friends!

What do you both like and dislike doing together?

What particular prejudices or biases do you share?

HOW DO YOU REACH A BALANCE IN PLANNING?

After discussing what you both like and dislike doing, you can begin to reach a balance between overplanning and underplanning. Reaching this balance may be one of the most critical factors in your trip's success and your well-being. Overplanning can deprive you of unexpected pleasures, but underplanning can lead to disorientation or disappointment; too many surprises can leave even a seasoned traveler uneasy.

On one trip we decided that for each city or town we would choose one museum and one church and allow one hour of shopping a day; we also decided not to devote more than a total of two and a half hours a day to those types of activities. With this limit, we found our choices difficult but rewarding. The sights we did choose became particularly important to us and we have appreciated and fondly remembered them in detail over a cup of tea even years later. Most especially, we discovered that by carefully selecting and savoring our experiences—rather than trying to amass as many adventures as time allowed—we were able to incorporate what we learned on the trip into our daily lives. Although collecting a variety of experiences can be fun, they remain only as souvenirs rather than contributing vitality and spark to our lives.

Each partnership needs to find an effective balance appropriate for both members. Of course, it's hard to specify exactly how much or how little is "just right" before you leave. But you can make tentative plans and regularly review them on the trip. Adjust your plans according to your day-to-day responses.

Discuss or write down what has been (on a previous trip) or what might be too much or too little for each of you on your next trip.

What do you both agree has been, or is now too much or too little? About what, if anything, do you disagree?

If you have disagreements, read the following sections for suggestions.

COMPROMISING CAN BE AN ART

When you make a satisfying compromise with yourself, you decide to give up something in order to obtain something more important in value to you. When partners make a satisfying compromise, each person's needs are taken care of and each gets something of value, rather than only one giving up something and feeling a martyr.

Some couples like and dislike so many of the same things, are in such agreement, or are so supportive of one another's desires, needs, and limitations that they rarely need to make compromises. Some people do not have the need or desire to control a situation or have their own way and can yield to their partners without difficulty. This chapter may not be particularly useful to such readers.

In other couples, both prefer that one member alone make the important decisions in a particular area. This kind of arrangement may work well for decisions about financial matters or redecorating the living room, but may not be as effective in planning a vacation. If you're part of a couple that delegates decisions to one member, you might want to consider using joint planning for your trip. Planning together can be difficult if you're not used to it, but it also gives you a chance to enjoy sharing ideas and working together. And if you've both contributed to the plan, you're each more likely to relish the trip's highpoints and accept disappointments without blaming one another. The vacation—its pleasures, surprises, and letdowns—will be yours, not his or hers. Of course, if one of you is a far more experienced traveler, the other may gladly (not grudgingly) follow his or her lead. You can both gain pleasure from the more skillful partner's plan. If one person does all the travel planning, the other can make contributions in another area of your relationship (doing business or career planning, house repairs, or reconciling bank statements).

Still others of you are sometimes too willing to compromise before even stating your position about your preferences. To avoid a disagreement, you may hold back your opinion or perhaps make a quick one-sided compromise. You may sense that any differences of opinion or any articulated compromises might threaten your relationship. Although disagreements and compromises raise more ripples than quick assent, learning to compromise can make a good partnership even better because each member states an opinion and hears his or her partner's.

You can begin by telling your partner what you would like and what you will offer in an exchange when your partner does not agree with you. You can then discuss what each of you is giving up and receiving in exchange. If you clearly tell each other what you want and make a compromise, neither of you will feel walked on. But if one person simply gives up, "It doesn't matter," when indeed it *does* matter, or if one-sided compromises are made too quickly the partner who compromises too easily may feel self-contempt for having compromised his integrity; he may strike back with subtle digs or criticisms of his partner or deprecate himself for being wishy-washy.

Satisfying compromises can be made only between two people who are committed to working together rather than hurting or one-upping one another. For instance, if a compromise leads to what turns out to be a regrettable afternoon, it isn't constructive for either to say, "See, ha, ha! I knew it! I told you so! My choices are better than yours."

Ground rules need to be established:

1. Enter the compromise situation with: a sense of humor, an attitude of good-natured give and take, and acceptance of the challenge in solving a common problem. Try not to feel you're embarking upon an unrewarding, heavy-duty job.
2. State your value, position, or idea and give reasons for why you think it will work, without making a personal attack on your partner.
3. Respect differences as expressions of integrity; use statements of fact, disagreement, or dislike. Restrain urges to: use disagreements as strikes against either partner, put down one another's ideas, discount or take away statements of difference, imply that your partner must change because you don't like his value.
4. Focus on the partnership gaining from the compromise in the long run rather than: manipulating your partner to come your way, making a sales pitch for your idea, bargaining ruthlessly, making the best possible deal, determining that one will be the winner and the other the loser.
5. Discuss what each may be giving and receiving in the compromise.

6. Set and maintain a time limit for discussing and making a compromise. Keep from becoming "Compromise-Over-Doers" or "Unsatisfying Compromisers." For instance: Essie and Ralph pride themselves in studying compromise to the "Nth degree." One morning:

Essie: Oh dear! It's my day for planning what we'll do and I see I've scheduled a special tour at the same time you said you wanted to go shopping. I'll change the tour.

Ralph: Dear, really, are you taking care of yourself?

Essie: Yes, I feel all right about it.

Ralph: Well, I really don't think so.

Essie: Yes, really it's all right. I made the error. I'll change it. Right now. I'll phone.

Ralph: No, you really don't stand up for yourself often enough when you really don't want to do something. You really need to think about that. And I don't mind doing it, really, I'll make the change.

Essie: No, really.

Ralph: You really need to be stronger for yourself.

Essie: Do you really think so?

Ralph: Yes, really.

(The conversation continues back and forth like this for another five minutes.)

Essie: Well, I really need to think about it.

Ralph: O.K. Take your time, I understand.

(After five minutes they begin again.)

Essie: Well, if you really want to, if you don't mind.

Ralph: Of course I don't mind changing. You *need* this one.

Ralph feels superior, a hero. Essie thinks she's been given something and is supposed to feel grateful but instead feels guilty for giving up her responsibility. Further, this whole "compromise" took twenty-five minutes.

7. When you make an agreement stick to it. Avoid playing a version of "Tricky Partner Fighting Game" by making an agreement just to get your partner off your back, knowing you're not going to follow through on it. Resist making an agreement and then trying to go back on it when other people are around, hoping that their presence will restrain your partner from complaining about your broken promise.

For example, Harry sits in a hotel restaurant, reading his newspaper. Wanda enters: "Harry, you agreed to meet me at Dino's at 10:00 and you didn't show up." Harry continues reading. Wanda raises her voice, stamps her foot: "Harry, listen to me. We agreed you'd do that because I did everything you wanted yesterday. I'm just furious." Harry looks up from his paper: "Stop acting crazy, Wanda. Sh-h-h." Wanda stomps out; on-lookers titter. One says, "Poor guy! How'd you like to be him?" Harry has elicited sympathy by his quiet manipulation!

8. Refrain from insisting that you have made an agreement when indeed you haven't.
9. After you've inadvertently made a compromise that left either or both of you feeling badly, focus on what you have learned from the experience to apply to another situation rather than blame yourself or your partner for "wrong-doing."

Setting Limits, Fines, and Rewards

Some couples make agreements about what to do to avoid breaking ground rules. For example, if you tend to make compromising a long, arduous task, limit your discussion to an agreed-upon time. You can even make agreements about what to do if agreements are broken. Partners who argue the terms of the agreements they've made can write them down at the time so that later one partner can't say, "I don't remember that." Part of an agreement can stipulate that a fine be paid by whoever breaks it: treating the other partner to dinner, doing extra chores, or an activity the other partner wants to do. Agreements can also include rewards (special celebration dinners or gifts) for both partners' keeping their word over a specific period of time (a week, a month, or longer).

Inappropriate Compromise

It doesn't make sense to compromise when:

- You are feeling manipulated or misused.
- Your personal or professional safety is threatened.
- Your integrity is at stake.
- You will lose more than you'll gain in the long run.
- Your physical or emotional limitations prevent you from making a compromise even if you would like to.

If you are used to making compromises, write or discuss with your partner one or two that have worked well for you. How and why did you come to make these compromises?

If this is your first experience in making planned compromises, each of you might want to identify just one or two things you might be willing to make a compromise about:

What wouldn't you compromise?

What ground rules would you use?

SPECIFIC AREAS OF COMPROMISE

If you like a particular pastime and your partner does not, there are several alternatives for compromise. You can decide to take on a sport alone or with someone other than your partner, not do it at all, or figure out how to make an excursion more palatable or even enjoyable for your partner. For example, Perry likes boating, I do not. We generally do not go on boating trips together, but I was willing to go on a ten-day boating trip without complaint because Perry agreed to find ways we could travel around islands and disembark for long exploration walks.

Activities

If both of you like the same recreational activity but one has certain limitations or dislikes, you can search for compromises that will avoid complaints or hardships. For instance, Perry and I both like to swim. But I like being in the sun and picnicking on the ground, while Perry can't be in the sun, likes a comfortable picnic table, and wants a room for changing clothes. So we always look for beaches with picnic tables, changing rooms, and a combination of sun and shade.

It is sometimes difficult to find these places, but with care and perseverance we do. At times I feel restricted by Perry's limitations, but then I remember my own. When I feel he is being too "persnickety" for me I can always write in my journal or draw a picture of a persnickety person instead of making comments that might ruin our time.

Perhaps one of you likes an activity that the other can enjoy watching while doing something else. Perry likes to go trout fishing occasionally, and I use the time to read, rest, or paint on the riverbanks, looking up from time to time to cheer him on.

Driving is an area of challenge for compromise. Perry likes to drive on back roads and I sometimes prefer freeways to shorten the trip if we have been on the road for a long time. We usually compromise so that one out of every three drives we take a freeway part of the way. This agreement also helps Perry avoid losing the route to the freeway.

Lunchtime represents yet another challenge. You can take turns choosing what each of you prefers, or make trade-offs for other things. If one takes his or her way without consulting the other, you can then decide to call it a gift or negotiate a trade-off. Lunch often involves compromises for us because Perry likes fancy restaurants, while I prefer picnics. Since Perry doesn't have time for restful lunches in restaurants during his business week at home, and since he can afford them and wants to celebrate his success in his career, I am often willing to accede to his desire as a gift (as long as he's willing to express his appreciation). Besides, I can't bear Perry's grumpiness if the picnics aren't just to his liking.

Here's another example of a successful compromise. Anna likes warm beaches, swimming, making reservations for accommodations, staying in the same guesthouse or inn for two or three nights. Carlos dislikes beaches and does not like to plan ahead for accommodations, preferring to stop when he feels ready and take his chances. He says that because he plans so much at home he doesn't want to plan on vacation or to have Anna make schedules for them. He also likes to drive long distances and wants to see as much as possible in the two weeks they have available.

This couple has several alternatives. They could ignore their differences and butt heads. Or Anna could decide to yield to Carlos and silently fume every mile of the way: "Why can't Carlos *ever* do what I want? Why do *I* have to do all the changing?" To console herself she might eat a huge dish of ice cream which would add to her weight that she could ill afford; she would become depressed. Or Carlos could decide to submit to Anna and whenever she made an error he would make a nasty crack, "Now see what happens!" Their third choice is to make an agreement that both could live with: Anna would make reservations for a three-night stay at a guesthouse or inn each week. They'd go to beaches not more than twice a week. Anna would drive further and see more each day than she originally wanted, as a special gift to Carlos. Carlos would give Anna some extra help around the house during the year.

Jack and Laura compromise by alternating "his way" and "her way" every other day. They take one another's limitations into consideration when they plan a day's activities together. For example, Jack chooses walking for the day and since Laura's limitations are no steep trails and a distance of no more than four miles, Jack plans a walk from one town to the next (one and a half miles away), with a stop for lunch and return. When it's Laura's turn, she chooses a museum and since Jack complains if he's there more than an hour, Laura plans for them to stay together in the museum for an hour, and she stays two more, while Jack goes shopping and reading in a café. They meet for lunch and go strolling by the river in the afternoon.

Write or discuss two or three activities that one of you likes and the other does not. Compare notes to clear up misconceptions and decide if or how you would like to compromise.

Travel Styles

Two people who have a great difference in travel styles need alternatives. For example, Stanton loves travel to foreign cities, while Leonore prefers quiet vacations in the tropics. Stanton makes the choice of places for a trip one year and Leonore determines the next. Mario and Carla divide their yearly vacation into two parts, with Mario making the choice for the first week or two, Carla, for the latter half. Whoever makes the choice is responsible for also setting up the plan, taking the partner's needs and limitations into account.

Sometimes one member of a couple likes tours, the other does not. Both Greg and Ernie can agree to go once on a day tour, but if Ernie hates tours so much that he will make life miserable for Greg, then he can choose another activity for a day while Greg goes on the tour. Taking a tour is also an alternative for one or both partners if you are inexperienced and want guides to take care of you. Disadvantages are that you may be given information you don't want, and taken to sights you don't particularly like. Further, you may have to wait for other tourists. However, if you do like the sight and dislike hearing lectures, once you have arrived you can visit by yourself while others are on tour. Or, if you prefer, you can rest, read in a café, or walk around nearby gardens and surroundings. If you detest waiting, be sure to bring a book, pen, pencil, journal, or sketch pad.

If you have a different travel style from your partner, what compromise would you make?

Time Alone and Time Together

How much time you spend alone and together depends on: how much privacy or intimacy each of you needs or wants, how different your style or pace is from your partner's, your interests and preferences, how much you like to fight or cause trouble between the two of you, your personal problems, and your ability and comfort in having periods of silence while you are together.

Need for Privacy. Is your idea of being together realistic? A "Romantic Dreamer," taking a vacation with her new manfriend reported, "We expected that by being together everything would be fine. It wasn't. I didn't take into consideration that I need time for myself. I've always known that, but somehow I thought I'd be different away from home. The all-American dream of 'togetherness' all the time is ridiculous."

"The Perfectly Happily Married Couple With No Problems" told friends before going on a trip that they would not have any trouble traveling together for a month because: "We get on so well at home. A few years ago we traveled for ten days together and had only one bad day. So this time we're going for a month." When they returned they moaned about having a really hard time. Where a weekend or ten days together might have been comfortable, a month was too long, without anticipating their need to be alone or with other people more often.

We have heard tales of couples who have lived fairly comfortably together for twenty years, but after returning from a long sailing trip have divorced. They were not prepared to live with one another in such confined quarters for so long.

If you are not prepared for the many changes involved in travel or the increased amount of time to be intimate, you may suffer rather than enjoy your trip. You might want to work out plans for spending some time together and some time alone.

How long would you feel comfortable traveling with a partner?

Under what conditions?

Differences in Pacing. Many partners have difficulty if one has a fast pace and the other is slower. One of the most common complaints is: "He [or she] goes too fast—just zooms from place to place—can't sit still for a minute—and all I want to do is rest after two or three days of a whirlwind tour."

Because moving at a fast pace is so much a part of our society or because vacation time is usually limited, many travelers want to see and do and move as fast as possible. Travelers who prefer a more leisurely pace feel inadequate for not "keeping up." Some cry, others get sick, still others blow their fuses as their internal circuits become overloaded. Of course, there is no pace that is "right" for all travelers, any more than there is a "right" pace for breathing, walking, or learning about fractions. One way to compensate for differences in pace is for partners to decide how much time each needs or wants to spend alone and how much time you need or want to spend together. For example, Anna and Carlos could decide that Anna would spend two days on her own—reading, walking, and resting on beaches while Carlos goes off to tour and see as much as he wants. Or they could separate during the day and meet for dinner.

Another alternative was devised by Scott and Ruth. Scott likes to keep moving from one spot to another every night, and every day he moves twice as fast as Ruth. If Scott goes at Ruth's pace, he only ends up trying to push her faster, "Hurry up! What's *taking* you so long?" But when Ruth tries to match Scott's pace she gets exhausted and bursts into tears of frustration. Yet they want to be together on vacation because they don't see much of one another at home. They agreed that Scott would cut in half what he wants to do in exchange for Ruth doing twice as much as she wants to do. Instead of changing their locale every night, they agreed to a series of two-night stays.

Different Likes and Dislikes. Some partners choose to separate at various times because they like to be independent or they have different interests. Occasionally, Perry or I go off alone on a stroll, shopping expedition, or swimming. Perry likes to spend more time than I do chatting with local townspeople and other travelers, so he does this without me. We often separate in churches and museums since we're not always interested in the same things and Perry likes to survey a number of objects or paintings, while I enjoy pondering the details of a few things. If either of us wants to do more than the other we agree to go our own separate ways for a while. Before separating, we make sure that we are each comfortable and safe (e.g., a nearby restaurant or well-marked hiking trail), and let one another know where we are going and when we expect to return. Despite any temptations, we hold to the agreed-upon time within ten minutes so that we don't keep one another waiting anxiously.

Safety is sometimes an issue, particularly for a woman in a foreign city. Such cases may call for special compromises or concessions. For example, Puffin is adventurous and has a faster pace than Murray, who likes to spend time alone in his hotel room. But Puffin is concerned about whether it's safe to walk alone to a nearby café. Murray could agree to walk with her to the café and return for her in an hour or two. Or he could escort her once or twice with the understanding that if she wants to go again she must find other people to walk with. Or Puffin might find it worth the taxi fare to go, and in exchange for Murray's willingness to accompany her some of the time, she can offer to do something that he would like. Of course, you cannot always make elaborate compromises in advance; you need to be able to handle differences as they arise.

Personal Problems. Sometimes partners need time apart to think about personal problems, to cool the air during or after a fight, or just to be alone. Perry and I go for fifteen- or twenty-minute walks when either of us feels annoyed by the other. If necessary, we just pull off the road, stop the car, and walk in opposite directions. We find this preferable to suffering in silence, putting each other down, or demanding concessions at a time when neither of us is ready, willing, or able to change.

Alone While Together. We've discovered the value of silence and allow ourselves the luxury of it for long periods during the day. Silence permits two people to be together but also alone. We have an agreement that either of us can say no to the other if we are not ready to converse or be interrupted.

We also always each have something to do if one of us needs to "be alone" while we're together; writing postcards or entries in a journal, reading, drawing pictures, watching people, or staring into space are our favorites.

Sandy and Gordon arrived at an appealing compromise during the following dialogue:

Gordon: I want to be together all the time. How about you?

Sandy: We'll get on each other's nerves terribly. How many hours do you really think we can manage?

Gordon: Four.

Sandy: I'll never make it. I need more alone time than that. I'd like two.

Gordon: Too little. Let's compromise on three.

Sandy: If you're willing to be together for one of those three hours in silence—when I'll read, putz around, listen to music in our cabin with NO interruptions. That means no questions, no discussion during that time.

Gordon: Agreed.

As you're making your travel plans, think about how much time and for which activities you want to be alone or together. You'll discover more, of course, while you're traveling. But be prepared to spend time apart, and be willing to respect one another's need to be alone at times.

If you choose to plan before you go:

How much of each day or part of the vacation do you need or want to be alone?

When are special times you want to be alone?

When are special times you want to be together?

If you choose to experiment with the amount of time you need alone and together on your trip, what do you expect to find out about your needs and those of your partner?

Travel with a Small Group of Family or Friends

If you have difficulty taking a trip with just your partner alone, consider traveling with a group of family or friends. Take time before the trip to plan so that each person's needs are taken into consideration. Such discussions, negotiations, and compromises are usually preferable to trial-and-error or bitter fights during the trip. You and your friends can spend several enjoyable evenings explaining what you each like and don't like doing together, discussing how you will support one another's desires and respect your differences, and planning for accommodations and activities. Even if you're best of friends, you might want to keep your first joint venture short, from a few days to a week.

On one of our early vacations with another couple, our friends insisted on having their bedroom on a separate floor from us, at opposite ends of the hall, so that each couple could have the privacy they needed to love or to fight without the fear or embarrassment of being next door. Such simple ideas can help friends traveling together remain friends.

Traveling with a small group of friends or family is an excellent alternative for couples who find it difficult or too intense to spend a long period of time together and for partners who have different interests. A couple can also spend part of their vacation together and arrange to join other friends or family for the rest of the trip. Or two couples can travel together in two cars, meeting for dinners but not committing themselves to entire days of togetherness.

Traveling with other people allows you to divide up travel chores and responsibilities and to share your experiences with others. But think twice about a joint venture if you tend to dislike being part of a group and having to take everyone's wants and needs into consideration. Similarly, if you dislike waiting for others or keeping others waiting or if you don't want to spend time forging compromises, group travel may not be for you. Only you can decide what you'd gain and lose by traveling with friends or family.

What additional needs and desires do you have to consider if you travel with friends and family?

What are your gains and losses in traveling with a small group of friends or family?

If group travel is not for you, discuss why not.

Your Limitations

Everyone has some physical or emotional limitations. And unless you and your partner are peas from the same pod, you'll have to make some compromises.

For example, Alicia has a bad back and cannot sit for long periods. Roger requests the first two seats in a plane because there is space on the floor where Alicia can lie down. In a restaurant she does exercises in the ladies' room. They like to hike together, but Alicia has to walk slowly, resting along the way. Roger appreciates Alicia's problem but wants to hike faster for part of the way. So he stashes a book in his knapsack, walks at a quick pace for an hour, then enjoys his reading while he waits for Alicia. If either of them feels it is not safe for her to be alone, then Roger tries to work in a brisker hike later in the day when Alicia is safely lodged at a restaurant or museum.

Even if you can't work out a perfect compromise, you can agree to be cooperative and not undermine your partner's efforts. For instance, if one of you can eat a great deal without adding a pound, but your partner is dieting, you can agree *not* to coax—"Oh c'mon. It won't matter. A little ice cream can't hurt. You can diet when you get back." It is a real disservice to try to talk your partner out of his or her need to care for physical or emotional limitations. It is equally discouraging if you try to nag your partner about his or her lapses. Such a conversation usually sounds like this: "Harry, the doctor *told* you to lose twenty pounds and here you are, eating your third piece of cake." "So what! I'm on vacation. I deserve some relief. Leave me alone." Of course, some people appreciate a partner who reminds them about overeating, but other people consider such reminders to be nagging, not care-taking.

Perry and I have had some of our most serious battles over our individual needs to watch our diets. We have sometimes tried to avoid the issue, sometimes labeled it an unresolved problem, and still other times made agreements or compromises. After many years of "I'll help you if you'll help me," "I'll help you, but don't you dare help me," "I'll help myself *and* you," and "I won't help you any more because you are not even trying," we have finally

arrived at a compromise that seems to work. Perry wanted me to stop him from eating and drinking too much and I wanted him to stop trying to make me order full menus to keep up with him. Perry agreed to pay me $10 each time he made a comment about how I ordered or the small amount I ate. Since he had such difficulty resisting this urge, I offered a reward of reading to him, telling him stories, or holding his hand while I waited for him to finish eating. With this system of a fine and reward I didn't have time to long for the food I couldn't have. Since Perry felt cared for by my comments and questions to help him limit his eating, I agreed to do so. If, however, he went beyond an agreed-upon limit, I would leave the table. As a reward to us both, after trying the compromise for a month, we treated ourselves each to a beautiful wine glass to add to our collection.

Each of you make a list of your physical and emotional limitations.

Discuss how you plan to cooperate with one another.

What compromises will you need to make, if any?

Behavior You Dislike in Yourself or Others

Talking about your dislikes of your own and your partner's behavior can be a sensitive subject, depending on how long you've known one another and how willing you are to talk without putting one another down. You might begin talking during a quiet time, over dinner in a restaurant, about one thing you don't like and want to do something about.

But direct discussion may be difficult if your partner will not even discuss the possibility of change or if you're too embarrassed to bring up an issue that is bothering you. For example, Jerry is always on time and Margie is always late. Jerry is too shy to tell Margie that her behavior annoys him, but he seethes about her to his friends. Jerry finally decided that it was easier to think about what he could do about the situation rather than try to change Margie. Since Margie is usually half an hour late, Jerry decided to always arrive half an hour after the time they set. If Margie ever arrives earlier, he might discuss the issue then.

You might begin a discussion by admitting one of your own behaviors—rather than your partner's—and ask your partner to help you decide what you can do about it, and what he or she might be willing to do to help you. You can also begin by mentioning behaviors you appreciate in your partner, and then discuss one behavior you don't like and have a suggestion for. You have to be willing to respect one another's need to refuse certain suggestions, and pushing for a change can often be more a hindrance than a help. Sometimes one of you will have to wait while your partner works through obstacles to a change. No one technique will always work for any set of partners; each twosome needs to decide how best to approach change.

If you already discuss your mutual dislikes of one another's behaviors, how do you do it?

Are you satisfied with the way you handle this problem?

If not, are you willing to make any changes? What changes would you make?

If you have not discussed your mutual dislikes of one another's behaviors and if it is appropriate for you, share one or two specific things you like and don't like about your own and your partner's behavior.

If you don't want to openly discuss such issues, what alternatives do you have?

If partners have parallel dissatisfactions with one another—if each partner is bothered equally—the trade-offs are clear and compromises can be made more easily. For example, Jack can't stand finding Laura's coffee cup in the bathroom with curlers lying next to it, rolling into his toilet articles. Laura can't stand to see Jack's clothes strewn over chairs and on the floor of the hotel room. Rather than ask each other to change the annoying behavior, they decide that Jack will pick up Laura's coffee cup and put away her curlers in exchange for Laura hanging up Jack's clothes. This form of compromise can work well for people who can say, "You don't need to change your behavior because I'll take care of what's bothering me if you'll do the same for yourself."

Some parallel dislikes can be resolved if each partner agrees to stop doing what the other dislikes. Laura could agree to pick up her own things if Jack will pick up his. This compromise reads, "If you change your behavior, I'll change mine." Other parallel dissatisfactions may be best left unresolved simply because partners realize that they need to have at least one area to complain about or disagree over (see "Perfectionism, page 56).

In some situations, even with parallel irritations, partners cannot make a parallel compromise. For instance, I used to be irritated and embarrassed by Perry's complaint about hotel rooms he deemed unacceptable (rooms facing onto a noisy street, or next to an elevator or cleaning supply closet). Perry was equally irritated and embarrassed by my complaints to the management about other guests' raising a ruckus at 2:00 a.m. Neither of us was willing to give up our right to complain, yet we didn't want to keep irritating one another. We had quite a few unpleasant scenes:

- When Perry complained about our room to the management, I glared at him in silence or whined, "Do you *have* to be so picky all the time?" He usually replied in anger, I will *NOT* be stuffed in these noisy rooms when I've paid my good money. The hotel just *saves* these rooms for people who are unsuspecting."
- When I called the front desk to tell neighbors to be quiet, Perry would hiss, "*Stop* it!" I was so angry that I would loudly mimic the neighbor's voices in hopes they would hear me, become embarrassed, and stop. Perry was enraged by my mimicry, "*Stop* it! You know better than that!"
- Once when we had a noisy room, I decided to *try* to be supportive of Perry and he *tried* not to complain. Instead he lay on the bed and sighed with exasperation at the noise from the Vespas. I asked—but in a mean tone—"Perry, are you comfortable in this room?" He answered, "No, I'm NOT comfortable," and continued to lie there, sighing. "For God's sake, *do* something to take care of yourself," I retorted. He got up, complained to the management, and changed our room.

By trial-and-error we agreed on the following: Whenever Perry did not like our room he could make a room change as long as he didn't complain to me or huff and puff in martyrdom, and as long as I didn't have to hear him make his complaint. For my part, I wrote letters of complaint, bought ear plugs, and wrote in my journal what I would like to do to those inconsiderate noisemakers but could not do without dire consequences. And we agreed that Perry would do more research on hotels in quieter, less populated areas.

Most partners most dislike their own and their partner's behaviors when either or both are anxious and have a strong need to control the situation. Though feeling lost in a strange place or having to cope with unexpected changes can make anyone anxious, some people are unaware of their anxiety or do not recognize their own efforts to control an uncontrollable situation.

Airports and planes seem to bring out people's worst anxiety-motivated behavior. In our earlier travel days, Perry complained about my battling my way through lines, accosting ticket agents angrily if I had to wait too long or if personnel didn't explain reasons for the delay. I used to give dirty looks to fellow plane passengers who drove me to distraction by gum popping, paper rattling, or loud talking. I complained to flight attendants, felt antsy sitting for long periods, and looked mean when I was squeezed in a seat for many hours between two people I didn't know.

After one of my own first business trips, Perry joined me for a weekend. I became anxious and flew off the handle at the airport when I couldn't find my return ticket. Perry offered to pay for a new ticket, but I wouldn't accept his offer and felt miserable and angry because I had not been able to behave as an independent, professional woman. Perry quickly learned to respect my need to fend for myself, by letting me pay for my own mistakes, and to stay away from me in airports!

This example illustrates the problem of nonparallel dissatisfactions—when only one of a twosome is bothered by the other's behavior. You have a choice of neither of you making a change or of one or the other changing as a gift to the two of you. In the case of my behavior at airports, I decided I could bear neither my nervousness expressing itself in such antisocial ways nor Perry's reproaches. I began to learn methods to control myself. I brought along what Perry called "security blankets": a novel, a book on sensual pleasures, ear plugs, sketchpad, drawing pencils, and watercolors. When I sensed my anxiety rising—but before it took over—I either wrote in my journal or grabbed a pencil and my sketchpad. I tried a technique I'd learned in an art class: without looking at either the pad or my hand, I made contour line drawings of people who caught my interest. I had the delight of being secretive and mischievous without getting caught because I'd look away from my model just as he or she was about to catch my eye. During the plane ride I'd add details or paint the line drawings. Perry and I were both pleased not only by the creative solution to the problem but also by the artistic product. I later exhibited my better work and sold some of my paintings!

But strangely enough, as I began to take care of my anxiety, Perry's travel anxiety began to show up more strongly. I realized that I disliked his getting to the airport hours early to get a decent seat, his constant floor pacing, looking frantic, overwrought, his complaining about crying babies, smokers, long waits, and poor service. At first we tried separating from one another in the airport. We met at boarding time at the gate, quite pleased about not having provoked each other.

It was a breakthrough when we accepted the fact that we were, indeed, anxious. We discussed how very difficult it was for us to leave home with our comfortable and familiar family, friends, and responsibilities. I talked about terrible catastrophes, that we might never return, die in a crash. I felt a loss of power and control because the pilot had our lives in his hands. Sometimes I'd promise

like a child, "Dear God, if you just get us through this time I promise never to travel again." We began to ease up and laugh a little when I recognized that it was easier to get killed walking out the door onto the street, or getting in the car and heading onto the highway each morning. Still, silent awful thoughts remained with me.

During long flights we began to touch one another on the shoulders, put our hand on one another's backs steadily holding it there for a while, or stroke one another's cheek in affection and comfort. Sometimes Perry could sleep right through lightning and thunderstorms and I was envious of his peace. Sometimes I wished he was awake to comfort me. I tried to read or if I couldn't concentrate I focused on breathing deeply and thinking comforting thoughts such as: floating in a pool on a warm summer's day, smelling flowers and the earth, rocking in a hammock between two trees in the mountains with a soft breeze blowing. At times I'd ask my hands what they would say if they could talk—one hand was my child and the other was my caring mother within me talking softly, comforting me.

I had been the one to begin making the changes, but Perry was the first to begin defining rewards for the two of us. He recognized how hard we had worked during the year and how much we had earned as our reward, the privilege of taking care of our needs as best as we could. When we traveled during tourist season, Perry made sure to phone ahead for seat assignments in the roomier first row. Instead of subjecting ourselves to long transatlantic flights from San Francisco, we made a one-night stopover in Boston. The ride from the airport to a hotel was short and relatively simple, and the additional expense was worth it because it allowed us to minimize our jet lag and preserve our humor and sense of well-being. When we traveled off-season we each requested aisle seats so we could move around more freely; that way we also usually had empty seats next to us for stretching out. I found a way to avoid smoke and crowds by sitting in the waiting room adjacent to or down the hall from our boarding area. Although simple, these techniques greatly helped us avoid behaviors that we disliked in ourselves and one another.

When do you feel anxious? When do you feel the need to control a situation?

How do you behave in these situations?

Which of these behaviors does your partner dislike?

Which of your partner's anxiety behaviors do you dislike?

How can you ease your own and your partner's anxieties?

Who Pays for the Trip

How you divide up the cost of your trip depends on your individual desires to go, the amount each of you can afford to spend, and your partnership's general agreements about finances. If you're equally looking forward to the trip and have similar travel budgets, you can split the expenses. Decide which items you will pay for together (e.g., airline tickets, meals) and what you will pay for separately (e.g., items of clothing, special dinners, a side trip).

If you live together and one earns a larger income than the other, you can decide, as we do, to put most of your combined income into a single pot, each reserving a specified amount for private accounts to be spent as you choose. In this case, the higher-earning partner must be freely willing not to lord it over the other how much more he or she puts into the pot. Some couples decide that the lower-earning partner will contribute to the joint venture by doing more tasks (making reservations, picking up tickets, taking care of baggage, tipping) before and on the trip. This method works best if both partners have an equal desire to travel.

Sometimes one partner wants to travel more than the other and can afford to pay for the entire trip. Before departing, that partner needs to realize that the gift of a trip may be ruined if he or she uses the gift as a weapon—"By God, I've paid for this trip and you better enjoy it"—or to control and manipulate: "I paid for the trip so you have to do everything my way." For example, Roy wanted to travel much more than Leann; he made all the plans and offered to foot all the bills. Leann felt that she ought to be grateful, but one afternoon she didn't want to do what Roy had chosen. He unfairly countered with, "Hey, who's paying for this trip, anyhow?" The next night she wanted to stay in her room because she didn't feel up to ordering yet another dinner in a foreign language. Roy was angry: "Look at all the money I spent to get here, and look at what you're doing! What's the *matter*? You don't appreciate all that I give."

Roy just assumed that since he was paying *all* the bills he was unquestioningly entitled to have his way *all* the time. Roy didn't understand how he was equating money with power, a dubious "gift" with many strings attached. Because Roy was paying, Leann felt obligated to follow along until she could barely stand another minute. Before they left home she might have saved herself had she told Roy she really didn't want to go on the trip, but was willing to give him the gift of her company in exchange for his paying for the trip. Her stipulation would be that she would take care of her emotional and physical needs without being demeaned.

By deciding who will pay for what before the trip begins, you can reduce the disagreements or resentments that arise from murky understandings about financial responsibility and the relationship between money and power.

Is your desire to go on the trip equally as strong as your partner's?

Who will pay for what on your trip?

Will the amount of money each pays into the trip affect your decisions when you have a disagreement?

What compromises will you need to make, if any?

How Much and What to Pack

Well-seasoned travelers have discovered ways to combat difficulties with baggage and what to pack; however, the less experienced may run into problems. Before you pack, you need to decide how much baggage you are going to take. Think carefully:

- How many pieces of luggage are you willing and able to cart around when you can't find a porter?
- How much money are you willing to spend on porters and taxis?
- Will you be patient at customs if an inspector asks you to open each and every piece?
- How many transfers from plane to hotel, or car to ferry, or bus to train do you anticipate?

Fights over baggage often occur when one partner wants to take more than the other, or when one accumulates more on the trip and expects the other to share the burden. When Perry and our son Mark went to England, Perry went on a book-buying spree. Accustomed to simply checking his baggage at one airport and picking it up at his final destination, Perry cursed every step of the way as he had to drag the suitcase of books at Dover, then onto a bus, then to the hovercraft, onto the train at Calais, and into a taxi on a rainy Paris day. Perry's subsequent shopping sprees have been followed by trips to the post office to ship things home, and he figures in shipping as part of his expenses.

How often we have observed travelers, ourselves included, carrying innumerable bundles onto an airplane, sniping at one another along the way: "Did you have to buy *that*? What are you ever going to use it for?" Some of these arguments could be avoided by an agreement that each partner will take care of his or her own excess luggage or offer the less-laden partner an exchange, "If you take care of my extra bags, I'll take care of settling the hotel bills and restaurant tips." Some partners decide that anything that the owner can't carry alone must be shipped home.

Many people detest the inconvenience and long waits at airport baggage carousels, so they limit themselves to one piece of carry-on luggage. Of course, this is practical only if your trip will be short, limited to one climate, and free of business or social functions that require varied clothing.

To avoid overpacking and arguments while packing, you can try to put aside any anxieties about how you'll look by picturing the situations you will be in and how you can be most comfortable in each.

To get a better idea of what kind of wardrobe you'll need, talk with people who have been to the places you're going or consult a travel agent. If you're still unsure, try what Eleanor and Anna do. They first discuss the activities they're planning and what shoes they'll need for city and country. Then each lays out clothes appropriate for each activity or occasion. They always lay out more than they need. Then each picks out three pair of pants, three skirts, three blouses, two dresses, two sets of underclothes, two pair of panty-hose, one dress for evening, one sweater, a raincoat, one pair of comfortable hiking shoes, one pair of comfortable flat shoes, one pair of comfortable evening shoes. For cooler climates they add ski underwear. All these items fit into one suitcase apiece.

Most travelers experience anxieties about lost or misrouted luggage. Be prepared: in your carry-on luggage stow toilet articles, medications (including an extra pair of eyeglasses), and any important papers.

What do each of you need to consider in packing?

Think about where you are going, how much baggage you can carry, how much you're willing to spend on porters—if you can find them.

Can you anticipate and head off arguments you are likely to have about packing or the amount of luggage you take?

What compromises will you make, if any?

If you don't need to make a compromise or already have done so, congratulate yourselves on solving this problem.

IMPASSES

Covert Disagreers deny the existence of a disagreement or don't verbalize their dissent. When two Covert Disagreers tangle they are likely to fight or disagree in a hidden way, saying all the while, "We both hate to fight." Neither compromise nor exploration of alternatives is possible for these partners, and no one, including themselves, can tell if they really want solutions. They may enjoy posing impossible problems for anyone who tries to help!

Other partners disagree that there's a disagreement. One partner says, "I see a conflict. You want X and I want Y. That's the way I see it." The other partner says, "I don't see it that way at all." When partners don't agree that there is a conflict, compromise is not possible. One alternative is for the partner who sees a conflict to do whatever he or she can do alone to remedy the problem. Sometimes dropping the issue (or partner) for a short time, a long time, or forever is helpful. Another possibility is for these partners to continue fighting—one overtly, the other covertly.

Partners who can agree there's a disagreement—who can verbalize and clarify the disagreement—are well on their way to discovering a satisfying solution, even if they cannot agree on a specific compromise. They can establish a method for handling decision making at those times. For example, Perry and I grew tired of continual impasses. We decided to use the following method when we agreed that we disagreed but couldn't reach a clear compromise.

Out of every ten impasses, Perry would get his way six times and I would get mine four times, but I would be able to choose *when* to use my four. We felt this was a fair balance: Perry cared about the higher number of decisions going his way because I'd taken too many in the past and he wanted more responsibility. I cared most about figuring out which decisions were of major significance to me. If I had four decisions that I really cared about then I felt in accord with Perry having the other six. We established a firm ground rule that neither of us could undermine the other's decision by derisive comments like "Ugh, that's an awful way to do things. I'd never do it like that. You'll see what will happen." However, we agreed to recognize the strength of our individual positions, to state why we disagreed as well as how we disliked our partner's having gotten his or her way.

As we became more comfortable with the plan, we kept a tally and began to laugh about ourselves. Perry would say, with a knowing look, "Oh here it's coming—I know—" and I would finish with "I disagree with you 100 percent because . . . but I will agree to support your decision." Decision making during times of disagreement became more of a game and a pleasure rather than a chore.

The ratio of six-to-four was appropriate to our needs at the time. You may find that another ratio works better for you. After several years I was willing to give Perry even more than six decisions out of ten if in exchange he would thank me for the extra decision as my gift. When he expresses his appreciation it stops my urges to undermine him by making jabbing, mean remarks, or complaining, "Hey, how come you won't give me my way when I give you your way so often?"

Some partners make other arrangements for impasses. Bernie and Annette use a rating scale of 1 (unimportant) to 10 (very important). When they reach an impasse, each rates the importance of the outcome. For example, when Bernie wants to go shopping and Annette wants to go hiking, they compare scores. If Bernie ranks the importance of going shopping as an 8 while Annette rates her desire to go hiking as a 6, they both go shopping. In contrast, Rayne and June don't have a rating system and don't want to keep track of how many times each gets his or her way. They decide that when they disagree, the one who wants something more than the other gets to make the decision. Both these systems have their pitfalls. Bernie could prevail more often than Annette if he always assigns a high number to his choice just to be able to have his way in a disagreement. Similarly, June could manipulate Rayne, who might retaliate in an underhanded way. Thus such systems work only if both partners are able to give a gift with no strings attached and if both have their needs and desires met in other ways. Each of you needs to decide how much time you want to spend working out a simple or complex arrangement for impasses.

Do you deny that you have disagreements but fight in a covert way?

Does one of you deny there's a disagreement while the other sees a conflict and way of resolving it?

If you agree that you disagree:

- **Do you want to continue your disagreement through overt or covert arguing or fighting?**
- **Do you want to throw in the sponge and go your separate ways?**
- **Do you want to try out a system of ratios in making decisions? If so: What ratio would you set up between the two of you? What needs would you have to consider in setting it up? What ground rules would you make? What might be the benefits and pitfalls?**

UNRESOLVED PROBLEMS AND PERFECTIONISM

Some problems between partners are bound to be unresolved before a trip. If you can identify them you can decide if you want to work on them while traveling, wait until you return, or not work on them at all. Our main unresolved problem is that Perry likes to travel more often than I do, and he doesn't like to go without me!

What is one of your pet problems between the two of you that is unresolved?

Do you want to keep the problem unresolved, work on it before you leave, on the trip, or when you return?

No matter how much you work, or for how many years, there are always going to be unresolved problems. No one can be perfect, and perfectionism may be the most intractable of unresolved problems. By perfectionism I mean the propensity for setting such high goals or standards of excellence that anything less than "top-notch perfect" causes displeasure, disappointment, or anger. For example, you plan a day and expect that every detail will go according to plan simply because you worked so hard to plan it. If your plan does not allow for any mistakes on your part or any divergence from the ideal on the part of the people or places you visit, you're likely to find yourself disappointed.

Striving for perfection is a loser. Perfectionism precludes humor, rest and relief, fun, and perspective. And since it is impossible to obtain, it is impractical! Although Perry and I are sometimes prone to fits of perfectionism, we knew that we could not expect entire foreign nations to cater to our sense of an ideal trip. So we tried to set realistic expectations in planning our visits to special places and meeting people of different cultures. We worked to balance efficient planning and allowances for spontaneity and the unexpected. Much as we tried, though, we sometimes fell into a trap and found ourselves on the road to perfection before we knew it.

We both dislike our inclination to demand perfection of the world and ourselves. Perry can become particularly disappointed when his plans go awry after he has orchestrated them so carefully. He tends to act like a conductor who flings his baton into the air while complaining bitterly and dramatically when his players don't live up to his expectations of them.

We are both in the soup together when our perfectionistic moods coincide. Sometimes I take too much responsibility for Perry's complaints or disappointments and feel they're my fault even when they're not! Even though I *know* it's unrealistic, sometimes I demand of myself that I be a supportive wife all the time, that I have perfect ideas for helping Perry when he is disappointed, that I always think positively without making any negative remarks. It is a great relief when I can laugh and repeat as a litany, "It's all my fault, it's all my fault!", or when I can write my self-deprecations in my journal. Reading these aloud later helps us both to laugh and appreciate the absurdity of our performance.

Every traveler has blind spots of perfectionism: unrealistic expectations of self, partner, and the trip. If you or your partner has perfectionistic attitudes at home, they are likely to surface more intensely in the unfamiliar surroundings a trip provides. For instance, at home Murray is a perfectionist about his day-to-day plans—so much so that he loses spontaneity. Puffin is bewildered and annoyed by his inability to just get up and go. Before their trip, they could try to anticipate Murray's heightened perfectionism about plans and try to reach some agreements or compromises.

What can you do if you want to alleviate perfectionism? One antidote is to give yourself and your partner an allowance of mistakes or errors that you will accept without recrimination. Complainers and Tantrum Throwers might allow themselves the luxury of complaining loudly and acting mean or nasty without guilt or apology once or twice a week. Map Navigators might allow themselves to lose their way once out of every three drives without berating themselves for their mistakes. Perfect On Timers might allow for delays on one out of every three flights without getting angry.

By allowing for a percentage of mistakes or a margin for error, you can accept or even laugh about yourselves and the situation when it lives up to your expectation—that it might not come off as you'd hoped. You can gain perspective and celebrate the fine things that do happen rather than focusing on pleasure-threatening demands for perfection. Of course, if you try to resolve *all* your problems you end up back where you began—on the road to perfection.

If you decide to make allowances for mistakes:

List your perfectionistic expectations.

Divide the list into three categories: expectations of yourself, your partner, and the trip.

Choose one behavior from each category and discuss what allowance each of you will agree upon for each item.

If you'd prefer not to tackle the subject of perfectionism, discuss why not.

DO YOU NEED TO ADJUST YOUR EXPECTATIONS?

After reading this chapter you and your partner might want to review your expectations of yourselves and one another away from home. Discuss whether you want to make any adjustments before your next trip.

3

Planning a Specific Trip

You have explored your agreements and potential disagreements, and have thought about alternatives, compromises, and unresolved problems. Now the two of you might make a specific plan for your next trip. How will you begin? Try writing a list of your needs. One couple might write:

- We are very tired after a stressful year—we need to rest and relax.
- Our interest and desire is to go camping.
- We'd like to visit our relatives to learn more about our family's history.
- Our budget is limited.
- We can be away from work for three weeks.

From this list, the couple might decide that since their primary need is to rest, they should not go camping, but rather stay in inexpensive bed and breakfast places and motels while visiting with various relatives. This alternative involves a trade-off between their interest in camping and their need to have a restful time.

What are your needs for your next trip?

What are your limitations?

How long can you be away?

What trade-offs will you need to make, if any?

SETTING A PLAN IN MOTION

Once you've decided on the general area you'll visit, how you'll meet your needs or desires, and the length of time you can be away, you're ready to set a plan in motion. How will you start? By contacting a travel agent, talking with friends, or reading books and magazines? Will you make reservations yourselves or leave it up to a tour or travel business?

Both Partners Ready to Plan

If you are both ready to plan at the same time perhaps you'll start talking together amiably at dinner or on a weekend stroll. If so, you can make a list of tasks and who will do what in the initial stages. For example, Joan and Harry have decided to visit Nova Scotia for two weeks. They want to rent a car and stay in bed and breakfasts, inns, or hotels. Joan will write to the Canadian Tourist Bureau in Halifax to request information on activities, road maps, and hiking trail maps in the province. Harry will go to a local bookstore and research hotels and bed and breakfasts in the area. Both will meet for dinner with friends who have sailed around the area and reported their delight with the unspoiled country.

After chatting informally and reviewing information, they list the tasks to be done so they won't have to rush at the last minute with too much to do:

1. Decide how many places to visit.
2. Choose hotels, inns, bed and breakfasts.
3. Write or phone for reservations.
4. Make plane reservations, ask for seat assignments, arrange for payment and delivery of tickets.
5. Make a chart or calendar of which places to visit on which days.
6. Include on the chart some possible activities in each area. (Research potential advantages and pitfalls).
7. Determine whether visas or passports are needed. (For this trip to Canada none are; U.S. citizens need only proof of citizenship—birth certificate, driver's license showing birthplace, or naturalization papers.)
8. Request immunization information. Get shots if necessary.
9. Decide what clothes to pack.
10. Purchase necessary clothes or luggage.
11. Find caretakers for: family, pets, house, garden.

12. Arrange for mail to be picked up. (Have it delivered to home if someone is there, or have it held at the post office.)
13. Line up transportation to the airport.
14. Advise police of departure and return dates, with a list of persons going in and out of the house.
15. Check up on last-minute details: plane reservations, seat assignments, time of flight, and the like.

Joan and Harry decide which tasks each will do, then write them on a calendar, spacing them out over a period of time. Each week they report to one another on their progress.

Division of Jobs on the Trip. As the time of departure approaches, they list their responsibilities on the trip:

- planning each day's adventures
- estimating time to drive from one locale to another or to an airport
- watching for and picking up luggage at airports and hotels
- tipping
- driving
- buying film and taking photographs
- buying supplies
- navigating with maps or guidebooks
- choosing restaurants and picnic sites
- buying gas
- arranging for possible car repair
- changing reservations (plane, car, hotel) if necessary
- changing hotel rooms if too noisy or inadequate
- taking care of anxieties and physical and emotional limitations

First Joan and Harry initial which jobs they would like and not like doing and divide those up. They discuss which jobs they'd like to do throughout the trip, which they'd like to trade daily and weekly, and which they'd prefer doing together. If either feels overburdened or guilty for not doing enough, they discuss the issue.

If you are ready to plan together at the same time:

How will you begin?

What tasks need to be accomplished?

Will you space out the tasks over a period of time or do you prefer doing them all at once, in a concentrated effort?

List the jobs you will have on the trip.

Which ones do you like and dislike?

Which do you want to do together?

Which do you want for a day, a week, or the whole trip?

How will you divide up your responsibilities?

One Partner Not Ready to Plan

What happens if one of you is raring to start putting a plan into action and the other is not? How can conflicts be avoided? It's possible for one to begin while the other takes his or her beginning protests to a third party to avert a battle.

In our case, Perry gets the travel "itch" many months before I've settled down from the last trip; so he begins his ritual by going to his desk after dinner with a glass of wine, taped music, and an armload of books, maps, and magazines. His initial phase continues for two or three evenings a week for three weeks. At this first sign of the new "travel season" my reaction is to roll my eyes to the ceiling and moan "Oh no!" So as not to hurt Perry's feelings, I quickly phone a friend to complain up and down about how upset I am that Perry is already planning a trip when I can't even contemplate leaving home. I don't feel ready for change; the trip might conflict with my job situation; and I've just gotten engrossed in my work. My listeners are usually sympathetic, but they always take care to recommend strongly that I follow six instructions:

1. Keep grumbles and protests for my friends, relatives, and my journal—*not* for Perry.
2. Write down my fantasies about the worst and best things that might happen on the next trip.
3. Wait and see what Perry comes up with.
4. Take a look at what parts of his plan I *might* enjoy.
5. Decide what I would go along with and what I wouldn't.
6. Consider where we might compromise.

My behavior each year is just as predictable as Perry's. I need to say "No, I'm not ready" while deciding whether or not I'm willing to go. During this phase Perry always knows to keep his ideas to himself, as he works them through; the part he considers most entertaining is how he'll present the trip to me. Once he appeared for dinner in a gondolier's hat because he wanted to go to Venice and was afraid I wouldn't like it since I'd complained of the heat and odors of dead cats in the canals many years ago. That year we compromised in the heat of summer to go to Venice for the day and spend the remainder of our vacation in a nearby village and in cooler mountain areas.

If you and your partner are not ready to plan at the same time, what will you do to avoid conflict?

Or, if you enjoy arguing and don't mind fighting, what will you get from it in the initial planning stage?

PLANNING BY YOURSELVES

Many partners like to leave planning details up to travel agents or package tour guides. Others feel that the time and effort saved by asking a travel business to make all the plans doesn't give them the satisfaction they derive from making their own arrangements. Trip Researchers enjoy coming up with ideas and then requesting travel agents to make trip arrangements, while Full-Trip Planners design all their own schemes and make all their own reservations. Though planning your own trip is work, there can be many rewards. Perry reflected:

> Planning the trip is like solving a mystery or being a designer, putting all the pieces together for a beautiful vacation. Rather than have someone sell me an idea or a package, I want to work on a trip to reflect our tastes. Knowing what we both like to do together is what makes it special.

Perry has a particular way of planning, which might be of help to those of you who have wanted to plan your own trip but were not quite sure how to go about it.

He starts by talking with friends about their travels. They often recommend a magazine article; for example, once from *Gourmet* magazine we gathered ideas for a trip off-the-beaten-track in Northern Italy with beautiful scenery, walking trails, picturesque towns, historic sights, and good food. Perry's favorite sources of travel articles are the *New York Times* Travel Section, *Gourmet*, and *Hideaway Reports* (which he found advertised in the *Wall Street Journal*). He especially likes to read a short article that points him to a source for more detailed information, often a bookstore in a small town. He writes for a series of guides for ramblers, and once it arrives, he can hardly wait to visit the spots he has worked so hard to discover.

Perry's next step is to find a map of the area mentioned in an article. Since villages are often difficult to locate, we have to wait until we can find an ordnance survey map in a bookstore. Then we excitedly call out, "Oh, *here's* that town we read about!" It's like finding gold.

After reading an appealing article and poring over maps, Perry phones a favorite travel agent to request information about hotels in a particular area. He also looks in bookshops, requests information from friends, or from European Michelin guides. He lists several hotels that sound inviting, then looks for their names in another guide book or article. If he can't find a second mention of a hotel he removes it from his list, not wanting to spend time and money on a potential disappointment. He usually chooses a hotel from a combination of recommendations from guidebooks, magazine articles, photographs, and friends.

It's difficult to figure out how long it will take to drive from place to place. Automobile clubs seem to assume that most travelers like to drive faster and for longer distances than we do. To gauge distances, Perry measures the squiggly lines on the map. On twisty roads he figures we can cover about thirty miles an hour. On freeways in Europe a driver can go up to eighty, but we usually travel at about fifty or sixty miles an hour. He adds an allowance for our getting lost or missing an exit. We have also asked friends how long certain drives take, but they also seem to like driving for longer stretches than we do. For example, a couple told us, "Sure, you can get there in a day, easy!" Fortunately, we planned for—and needed—two days. Coming from another direction, they met up with us, but they'd driven for ten hours with only a brief stop for lunch, and arrived looking like basket cases. We know now that when we're advised that a drive *should* take three hours, it will actually take us twice as long.

It's well worth it to figure out distances between one hotel and the next, and to research two or three possible stops for lunch along the way. Your ounces of homework can prevent tons of arguments on the road:

Caroline: Oh, you said we'd stop here (whining).
Hubert: I did not. I didn't promise anything.
Caroline: God, I'm starving. Let's stop here.

Hubert: No, that's not a good place. Let's try the next town.
Caroline: I'll be dead by then (glowering).

Even if you buy a picnic along the way, you can't rely on finding a spot that welcomes picnickers unless you know you'll be in the mountains or in country without fences.

When Perry plots our trip he takes the total number of days we'll be away and divides it so that we spend four or five days in each locale, with the exception of two one-night stopovers near airports. On a calendar he writes down where we're going to be each day. Once he has his first draft of the plan, he's ready to present it to me and to talk up all its selling points. By then I'm slightly excited and ready to take my part in researching, reviewing, and asking, "How far is it from here to there?" and "How long will it take to drive?" I help limit the choices and set about researching and listing possible hikes, excursions, and restaurants in each area.

Perry begins writing letters or phoning hotels rather than sending cables that somehow are transmitted with no return address so hotels can't contact us. Sometimes, if Perry wants to contact a hotel in a foreign country he asks a friend who speaks the language to phone for him. Phones are preferable to letters because he can make decisions on the spot. For example, if he finds no reservations available he can get a recommendation from that hotel or can look up others on his own. When he asks a travel agency to make hotel contacts, they often have to call back with, "We can't get you in one hotel you wanted to stay in, but we think we can get you into another." Since this process takes at least two weeks, Perry gets impatient waiting and would rather work out the details himself. When he receives a confirmation, he begins a file folder containing photographs and information on each place. He spends a good deal of time working out logistics and making last-minute checks on flight departures, since airlines or travel agents sometimes forget to advise of change of flight times or cancellations.

When our plans are complete Perry types and copies the itinerary and presents the first copy to me at a fine dinner I've prepared as a celebration. "The mystery is solved," he toasts, "the pieces of the puzzle all fit together."

What parts of your trip will you plan yourselves?

How will you make your plan?

How will you celebrate it?

What parts will you leave up to airlines or travel agent?

SPECIAL TRIPS OFF-THE-BEATEN-TRACK

Some travelers want to take trips off-the-beaten-track. Specialty travel agencies and college extension programs organize small-group tours to exotic locales; many of these tours are designed for travelers who want to pursue a special interest (history, cooking, athletic activities, etc.)

Among trips recently advertised in our local paper were a study group visiting a vibrant Creole culture with a 50 percent unemployment rate in the process of urbanization on the island of Martinique in the Caribbean; a river rafting trip through isolated canyons where Butch Cassidy had his hideout and where Indians carved petroglyphs; a trip from Quito, high in the Andes, down a dramatic road to the Amazon Basin for a dugout canoe voyage into country populated by jaguars, ocelots, monkeys, colorful birds, and aborigines. Patagonia beckons with glaciers, fiords, pampas, gauchos, granite towers, and black-necked swans. Or you can race across snow and ice by dogsled in Eskimo country, walk with a native plant expert over native grassland in California, take a camel safari to explore desert wildlife and picturesque villages in Rajashtan, India, travel through ancient Etruscan cities and necropolises, or ride mules into Death Valley in winter to escape the usual celebrations at home.

Or you can plan your own getaway: scuba dive off the Yucatan peninsula, trek for long distances in the Himalayas, examine bird and animal life in the Galapagos, sample the breads of Italy and the wines of France, or walk through Japanese bamboo forests and gardens during cherry blossom time.

Where would you like to go off-the-beaten track?

If you decide to travel to unknown territory would you choose to go with or without a guide or tour group?

PLANNING A TRIP TO A THIRD-WORLD COUNTRY

Travel to third-world countries can be exciting when you gain insights into a different way of life. You may be delighted by cutting loose from your society, like "floating vagabonds"[1]—enjoying the

1. Cynthia Ozick, "Enchantments at First Encounter," *New York Times Magazine*, Part 2, March 17, 1985.

quality of light of a new dawn in a foreign sky—becoming awe-struck by something so familiar far away from home, like a baby's scuffed shoe, a stone, a yellow bus, or a broken piece of glass bottle emerging from the mud after a rain.

When you and your partner take a trip alone without a tour group to unknown territory in a third-world country, you'll need to take more care in planning, avoid making assumptions, and develop special expectations. You may be going as a tourist to an untouristed area, to a country without information bureaus, American Express agencies, or even bookstores with maps and guides. Problems that typically arise in other countries are magnified in remote areas unaccustomed to foreign visitors. You will need to be realistic in assessing your own ability to handle extreme differences and accept certain limitations. For instance, you might enjoy strolling in an unspoiled village in Thailand or trekking in an isolated area in the mountains of Guatemala; but can you also accept the tropical heat under mosquito netting, or can you eat the same food for three weeks? Can you tolerate cockroaches in the best hotels or give up the luxury of using water whenever you please? Are you willing to take the necessary medical precautions? Or, knowing how much you like traveling alone with your partner, can you accept having to hire a guide?

After assessing your ability and deciding you are ready for your new adventure, research the customs and way of life in the country you'll visit. Think of yourselves as guests who have come uninvited, and adopt an attitude of friendliness with authentic interest, curiosity, and appreciation—without exploitation. Be cautious of overcomplimenting; say simply and genuinely that you like something. If not, the local resident may feel awkward rather than pleased, or you may be embarrassed when you receive the object of your compliment as a gift that you don't know how to reciprocate.

Harsh Judges who end their trip in a heap of complaints that the country they visited is "inferior" in order to maintain that the United States is "superior," may also be judged as rude and impossible by their hosts. Although third-world countries need tourists for their economy, some foreigners resent American tourists who can afford to live much better than the local workers who have built the tourist hotels. Therefore, try to prepare for waves of anti-Americanism without becoming defensive.

As in any foreign country, you can't make assumptions about inhabitants' ability to speak English. For if you assume they *don't* speak English you'll be embarrassed to find out they've understood everything you've said, whereas if you assume they *do* speak English you may be frustrated and disappointed to find that they don't. In any case, try to learn a few foreign words and phrases of the country you're visiting. Sign language, dramatics, and artwork can get you through many a difficult situation. Flustered in a restaurant without a menu, I've felt a rush of pleasure after drawing a picture of what I want to eat, then receiving a graceful nod of understanding, and finally the exact food I'd ordered. Nancy Braganti tells the story of her sister flapping her arms like wings, making a noise like a chicken, and making an egg shape with her fingers in an attempt to order hard-boiled eggs.[2] Maintaining a sense of humor and being sincere are critical to success in a strange new land.

You can expect business practices to be different from those at home. What may be inefficient or slow to you is a way of life for local townspeople. They have their own set of values and priorities, and sense of pace. For example, in some cultures a person's being late is a sign that he or she is successful. Similarly, the term "confirmed plane reservations" may not mean the same thing to small foreign air carriers as to large computerized American airlines. Don't assume that procedures for boarding will follow those at home. For example, Fran and Jean arrived at the small-town bus depot in plenty of time, bought their tickets, checked their watches and waited. Several buses left, and thirty minutes later they complained about how foreign buses must, of course, all be late. After an hour they discovered at the ticket counter that their bus had left on time without public notification.

In order to avoid misunderstandings you may need to read or ask friends who have visited the country you plan to visit. Misunderstandings can occur on nonverbal as well as verbal levels. For example, members of Arab cultures usually stand much closer when they are speaking to people than we usually do in the United States; this does not mean they are aggressive or disrespectful. Research will help you learn about greetings and manners, whether kissing the hand or kissing on both cheeks.

Before you travel, find out about other customs. Is it all right to eat with your fingers? Can women wear pants or must they wear skirts below the knees, as in the African republic of Malawi? What is appropriate head covering when visiting churches, temples, or shrines? Are there any local restrictions about the use of water?

2. Nancy L. Braganti and Elizabeth Devine, *The Travelers' Guide to European Customs and Manners* (Deephaven, Minn.: Meadowbrook Books, 1984), p. x.

How can you handle your travel funds, how do you use a telephone (when available) or post a letter or package? When and how are you expected to bargain? What are the proper procedures when civil war breaks out or if you are robbed?[3]

Sometimes American travelers change their attitude when they suddenly realize they can afford to buy more than ever before because goods are cheaper than at home. If you feel the urge to turn into an Obnoxious Rich American, control it!

If you plan to travel in a third-world country what will you need to take into consideration (e.g., food, insects, accommodations, need for a guide, willingness to be spontaneous, survival in extreme heat or cold, etc.)?

What is your attitude toward a different way of life?

OF WHAT TO BE WARY

In planning a specific trip you can avoid many disappointments by being conscious of areas in which you may need to be wary. The list here is a review of what we have discovered:

1. Be wary of airline offices or travel agents who may forget to tell you of change of flight time. Phone a week before departure, and reconfirm a day before.

2. Be wary of being assigned poor seats on a plane. Phone for advanced seat assignments, or get to the airport early during tourist season to have a better choice.

3. Buy earplugs and eyeshades to shut out "Yay-I'm-Free" travelers who use airplanes as rumpus rooms for becoming drunk, and who make frequent, loud complaints about "lousy service."

4. Be wary of airlines and restaurants that promise diabetic or salt-free food. Always carry emergency food in your pack or hand luggage.

5. Be wary of fellow travelers on vacation who suddenly want to spend more time with you than you do with them. Be prepared to say, "No, we'd like to have dinner alone, thanks for asking." Vacation is a time for you to do what you want to do.

3. Louise Purwin Zobel, *The Travel Writer's Handbook* (Cincinnati: Writer's Digest Books, 1980).
Ingrid Cranfield and Richard Harrington, editors, *The International Traveler's Handbook* (New York: The Dial Press, 1982).

6. Be wary of travel books and guides that are not up-to-date. Hotel and restaurant ratings change each year so buy the most recent edition. Since carrying many guide books is not practical, xerox and take along pertinent sections of books or magazines. If you accumulate too many books on your travels, ship them home.
7. Be wary of whatever might happen to automobile rental reservations between the time you make them from the United States and the day you arrive to pick up the car. To avoid hassles and delays, reconfirm car rental arrangements the day before you plan to pick up the car. Be wary of car rental agencies that suggest that you rent cars in large cities. In cities you might get around more easily and less expensively by bus, subway, or taxi. Rent a car just as you're ready to leave for the countryside.
8. Be wary of estimates from tourist offices, automobile clubs, and travel agents about the driving times between places. The distances may be too far for your comfort. Decide how far you want to travel in a day, week, or month in order to maintain your sense of satisfaction.
9. Be wary of arriving in a large city if you are driving there for the first time. Whizzing traffic can really upset you while you are trying to orient yourselves with map in hand. Stop at the outskirts of the city, and look for an empty taxi. Show the driver where you want to go on your map, motion to him that you will follow him, and pay him when you arrive at your destination. You may need to offer him a part of the fee before you start out.
10. Be wary of noisy rooms facing onto the streets. If your room seems to be one reserved for unsuspecting tourists, ask for a quieter room. If the answer is, "The hotel is full, I don't have another room," counter calmly but forcefully, "I have requested a quiet room." Often, the desk clerk doesn't want you to attract attention from other guests and says, "Maybe tomorrow." In the evening, talk with the clerk or concierge again to remind him or her of your presence. Most likely, you will get a change of rooms.
11. Be wary of concierges and clerks who tell you the only way to get to a place is by taxi. It is often more pleasant and cheaper to walk or go by public transit.
12. Be wary of signposts on hiking trails that indicate distances and average walking times. They are usually set for fast trekkers who don't want to stop to look at flowers, rest, or read. Take a pedometer to keep track of distances, so you can judge when to turn back.

13. Be wary of guide books that leave out important information like the locations of and seasons for mosquito and black fly infestations. Carry insect repellent in your backpack.
14. Be wary of innkeepers who extol the virtues of lovely waters for swimming, but do not mention leeches nor how to get rid of them. If a leech gloms onto you, rub coarse sand on it immediately, and it will drop off.
15. Be wary of locking yourself into a plan without an alternative. If you have your heart set on a faraway beach in Mexico, you need to develop a contingency plan if the "always sunny" weather changes to a ten-day storm.

What do you need to be wary of where you are going?

If you don't know what to be wary of, can you contact someone who might know?

DO YOU NEED TO READJUST YOUR EXPECTATIONS?

After working on a specific plan you and your partner might want to once again review your expectations of yourselves, one another, and your trip. Discuss whether you want to make any changes.

4

A Special Kind of Trip: Rambling

This chapter is for readers who want to ramble, or travel at a leisurely pace. Middle-aged partners may find rambling trips particularly appealing, though if you are younger or older you may find them equally enjoyable, especially if you have already taken all-encompassing overview trips.

Perry and I have chosen rambling as our favorite kind of activity because we love doing it together, and it is a way we can spend a month away from home, developing an intimacy and sense of well-being, as well as learning a good deal about the places we visit, ourselves, and one another. Our slow pace makes us feel sane, sensible, and satisfied.

Rambling is an activity for people of any level of physical ability who like walking in the countryside. There are groups and associations of walkers in Europe, one of which is the Ramblers' Association in England (1/5 Wandsworth Road, London, SW82LJ). The major purpose of such rambling associations is to help walkers enjoy their strolls and hikes in the countryside by preserving their rights through public paths on private property and by making paths walkable and easy to follow. Besides watching the condition of paths, the associations have also become a lobby group. They take special interest in long-distance footpaths and ordnance survey maps, suggesting ways of improving information of use to ramblers. Belonging to an association provides advantages for people who enjoy being guided by experienced leaders, with social contact and without worries about getting lost. Walking programs, usually on Sundays, vary in length to suit different capabilities.

Most ramblers who belong to associations or who walk independently usually define their pastime or sport as walking briskly in rain or shine, on full-day walks or longer. A true rambler defines him or herself as "gung-ho" or "keen on walking" great distances. We call this kind of activity "trekking" or "heavy-duty hiking." We have come up with our own variation of rambling and present our definition of what rambling is *not*, as well as what it *is*, for those of you who might enjoy the same kind of travel.

WHAT RAMBLING IS NOT

Rambling is not hiking, not walking hard or fast, not pushing to reach the tops of mountains, not planning too harshly nor too tightly, not expecting too much of yourself or your partner. It is sometimes not walking all the way to the destination you set out for the day. Rambling is also not careless or pointless wandering. Rambling does not include going beyond the bounds of endurance and interest of either person. For example, in rambling, you do not hear whines and complaints like, "How much further is it?" or "But how do you know it's only half a mile more?" or "Hey, you said it was only another half mile. When are we ever going to get there?"

WHAT RAMBLING IS

Rambling is wandering in a caring and pleasurable way over the countryside, walking at a comfortable pace. Rambling is a good excuse to stay longer in a place that you might have once driven through quickly on the way to a major sight, saying, "I'd love to come back here." Rambling can be a walk in the mountains, or from a village to a town with a daypack on your back, an ordnance survey map in your pocket, a strong insect repellent, a pair of worn and comfortable boots or shoes, a Gortex parka or windbreaker, and Gortex pants in case of rain. Rambling can become "rumbling" (or rambling on wheels) if done on a bicycle, or by car, driving for short distances, stopping along the way as you please for a stroll or a visit to a church, for shopping, eating, or chatting.

Rambling is a way to discover what exists in the world and your responses to a place and its people (or lack of them). There is time to think about how you have assimilated your past into your present, and to dream of your future. Rambling gives you time to appreciate your good humor or lack of it, and to rest before it gets worse. It gives you time to become aware of as much as you please, to have the luxury of changing your mind, to stay longer in a spot that offers you sudden surprises and delights. Rambling includes both the excitement of discovery and the simple rewards of ice creams, teas, wines, shops, people, and sights. Rambles allow for spontaneity, but a spontaneity that reflects planning—so you know how high the climb or descent, how long a walk from one point to another, and how such details fit your and your partner's desires, strengths, and limitations.

If rambling is the kind of travel you like to do, you can decide whether you want to and can afford luxury accommodations in areas where you can take half- to full-day rambling trips or if you want to go to bed and breakfast places, camping, or to youth hostels in the same area. Rambling is for people of any income.

THREE RAMBLING TRIPS

The following brief descriptions of daytrips in the countryside, towns, sights, and restaurants do not include information typically found in guidebooks, historical pamphlets, or on ordnance survey maps. Rather, these excerpts from our travel journals illustrate the flavor of a way of travel that you and your partner can apply to trips in this country and abroad. They also can serve as an example of a style of vacation writing that you might enjoy.

You could take parts or all of the same daytrips as we did or modify them to fit your own needs, desires, and budget. If you want to hike more rigorously than we did, head for the more difficult trails in the same areas or hike to nearby towns. If you don't want to ramble as often as we, you can drive to sights, shop, or rest. Although we rented a car to go from one rambling spot to another in the same general area, you can also go by train or bus. Hotels and restaurants may change management and quality from year to year but the walks, the special ways we explored will remain as models which you can adapt to suit yourselves.

Trip 1: The Cotswolds and Devonshire Moor of England

We chose England because Perry feels that this is the home of all ramblers. Major walks are listed in each area by the Ramblers' Association or Automobile Association (AA), and minor walks are published by village church societies and local bookstores. Many, many books describe the delights of English walking. The trails are all posted, the walks between villages are close and not steep, and the language barrier is minimal. Sights of historical interest are everywhere—castles, ruins, churches, national trust houses, and gardens. "Rumblers" can drive short distances from one special spot to the next, and the scenery changes rapidly from London to the Cotswolds, to Devon, and so on. The climate is neither too hot nor too cold. Since England offers so much, we could choose one area as a center, from which we could ramble each day, and return at night.

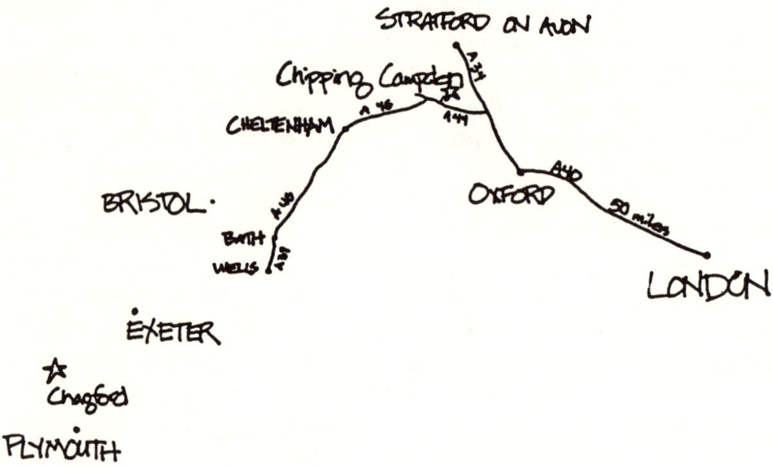

Day 1. Chipping Campden to Mickleton to Hidcote Gardens and Bartrim, to Broadway, to Chipping Campden.

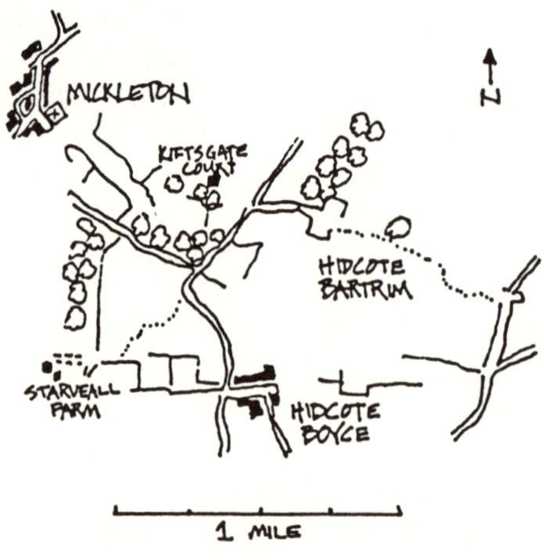

Drive from Chipping Campden to Mickleton—3 miles
Walk from Mickleton church parking lot to Hidcote Gardens and Bartrim—1 1/2 miles[1]
Lunch: *Hidcote Gardens*
Return walk from Hidcote through lower gardens, to Mickleton
Drive to Broadway—6 miles
Tea: *teashop in Broadway*
Drive to Chipping Campden—5 miles
Dinner: *Kings Arms Hotel, Chipping Campden*
Hotel: *Kings Arms*

We're sitting in the garden of the Kings Arms Hotel, under a blue umbrella, next to some beautiful climbing, perfumed pink roses, on green grass, surrounded by the yellows of the Cotswold stone houses and slate roofs. I'm eating raspberries and nectarines bought from a neighboring farm.

Today we walked by the church, cemetery, and little shops in Chipping Campden before driving to Mickleton, three miles away. Parking in back of the church, we began our walk through farmland to Hidcote Manor and Bartrim. The grass grew over the footpath along the route, so we imagined the property owners didn't want thoroughfares too close to their own houses and gardens. The Ramblers' Association hadn't yet cleared the way. Feeling slightly off-course, I climbed over a fence, and Perry tumbled over, a little like Peter Rabbit. A kindly gardener showed us how to get through; however, just as we were about to leave the property, the lady of Kiftsgate Garden Manor blew a gasket. She shouted, "How did you get in? You *must* know you trespassed! If you can't follow a map then don't use one; don't come at all. Don't you know an English gentleman's home is his castle, ahem, I mean his castle is his home!"

Perry says he'd love to send the woman a letter on engraved stationery saying he hoped he could do the same for her at home. Oh dear! It is very unusual for Perry to trespass, and this time he didn't even know he'd done it.

We had tea in Hidcote Gardens, walked through the lovely village of Hidcote Bartrim and returned through the bottom of the gardens. Pausing to observe the flowers and their visitors, we delighted in two rose lovers bending over, writing down the names of

1. Note: Avoid walking through the back entrance to Kiftsgate Gardens; it is private property, and the owner shouts!

their favorite specimens—together with glasses falling off the bridges of their noses at the same time.

Leaving the gardens through fields of sheep and grain, we rambled downhill by a stream. Yellows, greens, and blues, like Turner paintings, encircled me with the same quality of misty light that he was able to capture. I was thrilled.

Arriving in Mickleton, we drove to Broadway—a tourist town now, crowded with antique stores and shops too cute for us, and many people weaving in and out. On the return trip to Chipping Campden, Perry nervously practiced driving on the left side of the road, afraid we'd hit the right side of parked cars. We didn't.

Back in Chipping Campden, we walked through town and I took out my paints in our hotel room, and tried a watercolor of a street scene. I didn't like the results. I often get disappointed when I can't paint the beauty that I see, felt I was trying to do too much. So, when awash with too much that's beautiful, I looked around to find a contrast for balance and settled today on observing particularly pale and flabby travelers on the streets below.

Our wonderful hotel, the Kings Arms, has only 10 rooms, only a few with a private bath, excellent food. We had fresh, very fresh vegetables grown locally, tiny corn on the cob, and Scottish salmon—pale pink, and tasty.

Day 2. Chipping Campden to Snowshill to Tewkesbury to Haile's Abbey to Chipping Campden.

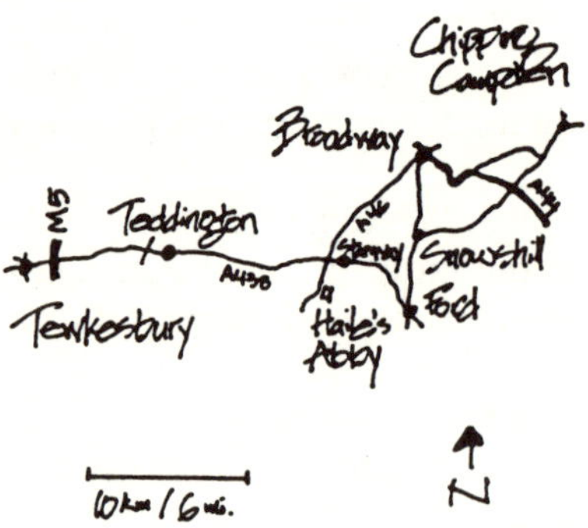

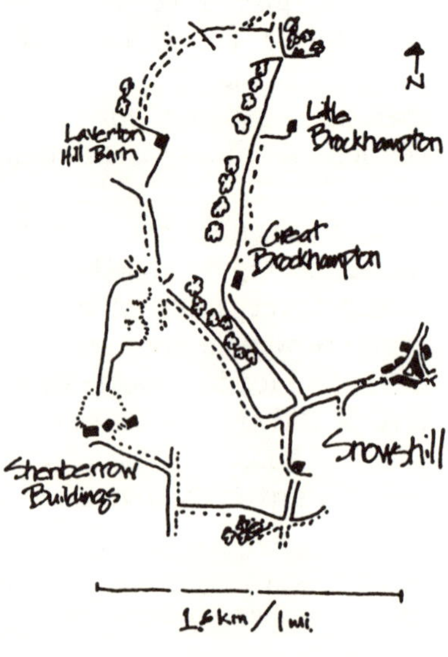

Drive from Chipping Campden to Snowshill—7 1/2 miles
Walk from Snowshill and back on a loop trail—4 miles
Lunch: *Snowshill Trust House Pub and Garden*
Drive from Snowshill to Tewkesbury—17 1/2 miles
Tea: *Hop Pole Gardens by the Severn River, Tewkesbury*
Drive from Tewkesbury to Haile's Abbey—13 miles
Drive from Haile's Abbey to Chipping Campden—13 miles
Dinner: *Kings Arms Hotel*

After breakfast today we consulted an ordnance survey map and drove to Snowshill, a lovely Cotswold village. Walking on a country road above the town and across it, we enjoyed the beauty we had stumbled upon. I collected flowers—wild roses, forget-me-nots, Queen Anne's Lace, buttercups, and lavender and purple nameless ones. We came upon a class of well-behaved school children hiking up from Broadway with their master, and paused to chat with three exhausted girls on a three-day Duke of Edinburgh excursion. Hot and sweaty, they leaned against one another telling us how sorry they were they'd taken on this 10-mile-a-day trek. How glad we were to be rambling.

Back at Snowshill we admired a beautiful 16th-century Tudor house with a hideously over-decorated interior. The garden was delightful and the sun shone. In the pub Perry had a terrible looking "cottage pie" and I had cold turkey. I couldn't resist sketching an English woman leaning over to gossip intimately with a friend—her mouth spread thinly across her teeth, her eyelids held in the shapes of banana crescents.

We drove to Tewkesbury, where 21 years ago, I remember history coming alive for the first time, when I read a novel about the War of the Roses on the very spot where it was fought. This time in Tewkesbury I really wanted to visit an abbey. At last! I've waited so long to *want* to see a sight rather than feel obligated to. Perry and I both loved being in Tewkesbury Abbey, a great, gray 12th-century Norman stone structure. Inside, a giant vase containing Queen Anne's Lace, mauve Persian lilies, and blue lupines beautifully contrasted with a marble sarcophagus on which was carved a decaying skeleton with a snake and snail at his toes and a mouse eating his guts. People of medieval times really knew their God and Devil in a much earthier way than most people I know today. Their work appeals to my senses.

Outside, we walked along the streets window-shopping, and as we looked at one another, each a mirror of the other's tiredness, we stopped for tea at the Hop Pole Hotel garden on the banks of the Severn. Afterwards, with a surge of new energy, we spontaneously agreed to stop at the ruins of Haile's Abbey on the way back to Chipping Campden. Although this meant breaking our general rule to visit no more than one church or museum a day, we reasoned that since we walked all morning we had earned an extra one. The tiny 12th-century church across from Haile's was a wonderful surprise of medieval frescoes. We would never have thought to go there had we not met a local gentleman on the path who was most eager to share his love of the church and its history. I edged away, fearing I'd be taken over by a compulsive talker who would tell me facts, when I simply wanted to sense being there alone. Perry, however, was delighted. Not only did he learn some history, he got some very good tips on where to visit another day—Stanton, Stanway, and Winchcombe, all unspoiled towns.

Upon leaving the church we strolled through the grass-carpeted ruins of Haile's Abbey. This really was a treasure, an unexpected find—worth going beyond our usual limits. Spontaneity today would never had developed in such a delightful way had we not planned for it! We would have been arguing, fighting—not able to appreciate a day like today.

Perry is still nervous about driving but I pat him on the back occasionally. He stubbornly resists giving up the wheel or control—to me. Fortunately, I didn't mind. Back at the Kings Arms we did our daily laundry and slept for two luxurious hours before a delicious dinner of smoked salmon, beautifully prepared sole, fresh vegetables, and charentais melon. Why aren't melons at home as small and sweet?

Day 3. Chipping Campden to Winchcombe to Sudeley Castle to Stanway to Chipping Campden to Stratford-upon-Avon to Chipping Campden.

Drive from Chipping Campden to Winchcombe—10 1/2 miles
Walk from Winchcombe to Sudeley Castle—1 mile
Lunch: *Sudeley Castle*
Walk from Sudeley to Winchcombe—1 mile
Drive from Winchcombe to Stanway—5 miles
Drive from Stanway to Chipping Campden—5 1/2 miles
Drive from Chipping Campden to Stratford-upon-Avon—10 1/2 miles
Dinner: *Shakespeare Theater, Stratford*
Drive from Stratford to Chipping Campden—10 1/2 miles

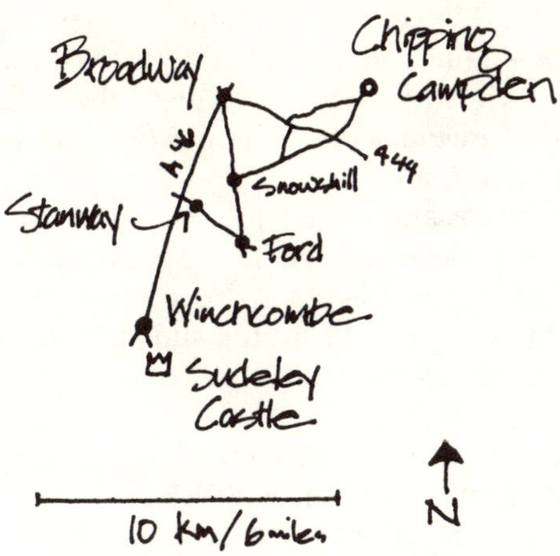

I woke up with my back aching, remembering an awful dream about returning to teach school and finding a disarray in the classroom with a group of children who said they wanted to help but instead created a chaos and wouldn't stop; I lost control. I think this nightmare in some form occurs each year for classroom teachers everywhere.

We were the last to arrive at breakfast at 9:00, after which we strolled into the old covered woolhouse market right in front of our hotel. Girl guides' mothers had a bake sale and we bought flowers in tiny woven baskets. Perry found a treasure trove of guidebooks and ordnance survey maps illustrating footpaths through fields.

We decided to follow recommendations from the gentleman we met at Haile's Abbey yesterday, choosing a town, a walk to a castle, and later to the theater. We seem to be majoring in lesser abbeys, castles, and homes loved by the Cotswold people and unknown to many tourists. Visitors seem to be local folks on day outings with their families. Winchcombe was a wonderful town, bustling with the daily activity of people who lived and worked there. A certain pride and authenticity was in the air, which is absent from towns exploited by tourists. We wandered down the streets, and from the town rambled to Sudeley Castle, a fine small 12th-century structure, part lived in, part in ruins. To our surprise and pleasure a regiment wearing 17th-century costumes marched past us and we watched them changing guard.

Entering the courtyard, my eye immediately chose the panes of Flemish glass windows, filled with figures of monsters and ladies with large breasts carrying fruits. How sensual and earthy are their expressions of agony and ecstasy! We decided to limit our viewing to just one part of the interior—a fine museum of antique toys; the only one I've ever seen better is in York. I especially loved the dolls made of lobster claws and furniture made of wishbones (which I've collected for years but never found a use for).

England has such nice tea rooms and buffets in castles and trust houses, so we had lunch and Perry fed the ducks in the pond. Slowly we meandered back to Winchcombe town and drove a few miles to discover Stanway and Stanton, both beautiful and unspoiled towns with tiny Norman churches. How much we'd love to rent a cottage here some day!

Back in Chipping Campden for tea and ice cream, I hugged Perry and announced, as do my students, "Oh, this is VERY fun!" Suddenly I realized I'd rather not go to Stratford as we'd planned for the evening. I'd had enough and wanted to savor our beautiful day; just one more good thing might pull me over into ill humor. But Perry had gone to the trouble of sending for the playbill ages before we left home, picked out a date, sent money in English pounds for the tickets, overpaid and made a donation to the Shakespeare theater. Besides, our hotel concierge had worked in advance to get us excellent seats. So, not wanting to disappoint Perry, I gave the decision to him.

Later . . . I'm not sure what made that trip to Stratford worth it for me but I think it was a combination of the new and excellent production of *Midsummer Night's Dream* and Perry's delight in the results of his careful planning for tickets. On the way back to Chipping Campden, however, I felt my circuits overloaded and noted that my face grew pinched and my voice nasty. Too much is just too much for me. Perry, though, was thrilled.

Day 4. Chipping Campden to Broad Campden and return, to Compton Wynyates to Shipston-on-Stour to Chipping Campden.

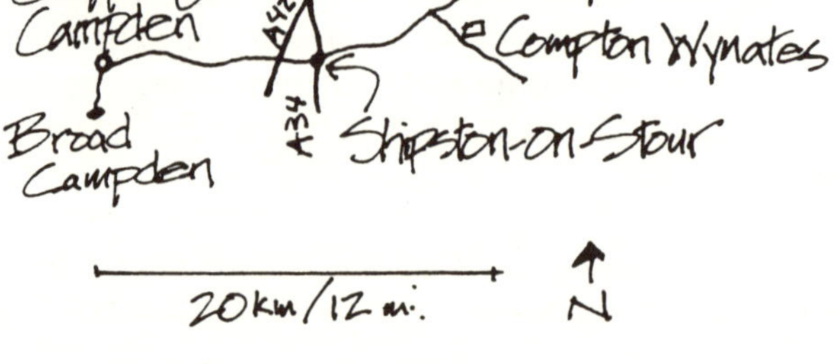

Day 5. Chipping Campden to Lower Slaughter, to Upper Slaughter and return, to Stow-on-the-Wold, to Moreton-in-Marsh to Chipping Campden.

Day 6. Chipping Campden to Bath to Wells to Chagford, Devonshire.

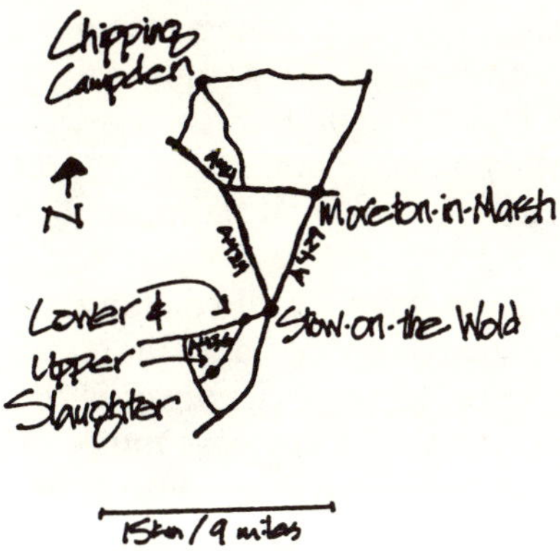

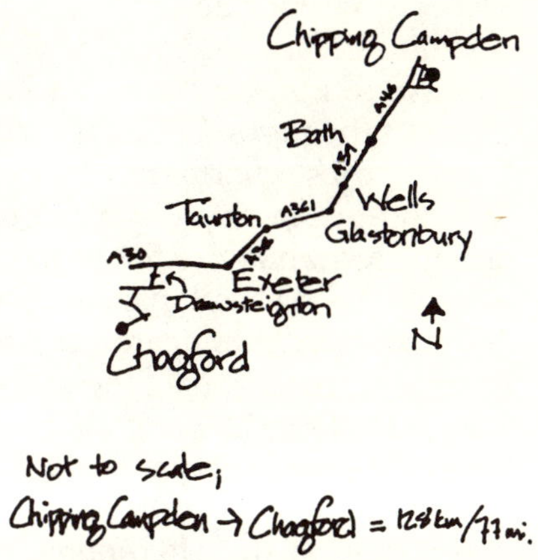

Drive from Chipping Campden to Bath (via Snowshill, Stanway, Winchcombe)—60 miles
Drive from Bath to Wells—21 miles
Lunch: *Swan Hotel, Wells*
Drive from Wells to Chagford (via motorway)—77 miles
Dinner and Hotel: *Gidleigh Park Hotel*

We were very resistant to leaving the Cotswolds, even though one of the last two days was not a great one. It was time for a few mistakes. We had a good walk by footpaths from Chipping Campden to Broad Campden and back by way of the nettled woods, and drove to a magnificent house and gardens, closed to the public; we hadn't checked our national trust house brochure to find which were open on which days. Sunday lunch, with no choice other than the menu at the Prince George Hotel in Shipston-on-Stour was singularly terrible—gray salmon with thick, floury whitish-gray sauce, gummy gray mashed potatoes, limp overcooked gray-green string beans, and a gray-looking pudding. I repressed my huge desire to say, "See, I told you so. If you'd only listened to me and gone on a picnic this would never have happened!" I managed, instead, to tell Perry how much I appreciated his fine choice of the Kings Arms, how this was the first pale and pasty food we'd had, and how the food used to be so consistently poor in England twenty years ago.

Our last day was a delightful one—a short drive to Lower Slaughter and a walk to Upper Slaughter, lunch at Lord of the Manor House in the garden, and return to Lower Slaughter by a beautiful stream bordered by weeping willows. Shakespeare must have chosen this one for Ophelia's drowning. We stopped for ice cream at the post office by the mill and drove on to Stow-on-the-Wold, a most charming town with great antique stores. Tea in Moreton-in-Marsh was a pleasure, and we enjoyed sharing at dinner our recounting of the past few days.

Both of us felt both pain and pleasure as we'd walked along the last day, sometimes apart and sometimes holding hands; it was a bittersweet time of happiness now mingled with memories of the past when life was not good for us. Perry told me how much he loved our days walking in the mornings, stumbling upon something of historic or horticultural interest, eating, shopping, tea-ing and resting in the afternoons. I loved picking flowers on every walk—combining colors and fragrance into a bouquet of blue geranium, moss rose, and lavender wild ones; reading a book on dyslexia, lying on the grass on top of a hill surrounded by sheep high above a town with a church below; walking the same paths as characters in novels, admiring Norman naves; thinking about being a nobleman having to lose my privacy by opening my castle-home to the public to keep up my property and image; trying out British accents; and staring at fascinating faces. How true is my mother's adage about people and art: "ugly can be beautiful, but pretty will never make it."

We knew we didn't want to leave the Cotswolds when Perry got lost, I think on purpose. He kept insisting on not taking freeways even after asking me to direct him. At those "wrong turns" when I shouted out, "NOT there!" he chirped along saying how pretty the road was. I hated the frequent brake-jamming with the road so narrow for so long, and I wanted to drive. I decided to compromise when Perry stubbornly refused to budge from the wheel, and said I didn't like his unwillingness to give me control when I wanted it as much as he did! I requested three minutes of time when I could make nasty remarks without reproach, and with Perry's agreement I thoroughly enjoyed my complaints. After two and a half hours my back was aching and he was most willing to stop—a great relief since I remember terrible times in my childhood when my father persisted in driving on, until I vomited from motion sickness—and then he lost his temper.

We made it to Bath in three hours and loved seeing the buildings laid out in crescents in that beautiful city. Walking in the streets is aesthetically delightful, the light translucent. Since we didn't want to take in more than we could handle on a travel day, we avoided a visit to the Roman Baths and Pump Room which we'd seen twenty years ago and were disappointed—not nearly so grand as we'd expected. Instead, we strolled into a few antique stores with prices too high and quality inferior to Winchcombe and Tewkesbury.

On we drove to a "bar lunch" at Swan Hotel in Wells, where we were fascinated by two British ladies, carrying on a conversation full of non sequiturs. Each had an attitude of all-knowing. While one was talking, the other seemed to be changing the subject or preparing a rebuttal. Each said, "Yes, yes" to everything; sometimes to agree with what she herself had just said, other times to pretend agreement with her partner, and still other times to convince her partner that she was listening when indeed she wasn't. During our eavesdropping I wrote:

Number 1: In that painting (on the wall of the bar) she looks mahvelously photogeenic.

Number 2: Yes, yes.

Number 1: I don't know what I shall do. I don't like this dress I threw on today. You know when you don't like something it will never wear out. Well, Cordelia was going to make these pair of bloomers and they'll be out of fashion before she finishes. Absolutely absurd, don't you know.

Number 2: Yes, yes . . . yes, yes . . . yes. Have you ever had the fizzy water from France, the kind you push on the leever?

Number 1: No, yes. I never have any fizzy water.

Number 2: Well, people pop in and I have to have something.

Number 1: Yes, yes, I must try it some time.

Number 2: I send for it. I send for anything. I ordered a chicken from Barker's. It was tough as 'ell. It ought to be good.

Number 1: Yes, yes. I don't eat grapefruit because it's awfully acid. I have orange. I get my own things, you see. The exercise is good for me.

Number 2: Yes, yes.

Number 1: Yes, yes.

Number 2: If I know somebody's coming I always have some.

Number 1: "Yes, yes."
Number 2: "That *is* a rather engaging painting." (She looks again on the wall of the bar.)
Number 1: "Yes, yes."
Number 2: "Well, time to go."
Number 1: "Yes, yes."
(Both exit).

How wonderful it is to take time to appreciate the absurd, ridiculous in life; it gives us perspective again.

Wells Cathedral was magnificent. I tried to draw the inverted arches, but they resembled an angry owl. As we left Wells I asked Perry in good humor if he wanted to continue stubbornly driving along tiny, picturesque roads which would mean arriving very late in Chagford, or if he was willing to save a lot of time on a motorway. Hooray! He chose the latter, *my* way, and we arrived at Chagford by 4:30—eight hours door to door. We had tea on the edge of Dartmoor forest, alongside flowering rhododendrons, and dinner at Gidleigh Park—too pretentious for me, but Perry was pleased. I don't like food so outdoing the Cordon Bleu—sauces too perfectly colored, too perfectly placed on the plate, too perfectly divided into neat halves. I don't really like the idea of being ushered into a dining room and having the door closed on the room. I was reminded of feeling hemmed in with formality at my grandmother's, not able to breathe—air too holding and close, a forced intimacy with no way out.

Day 7. From Chagford to Fingle Bridge to Castle Drogo to Fingle Bridge to Drewsteignton to Chagford.

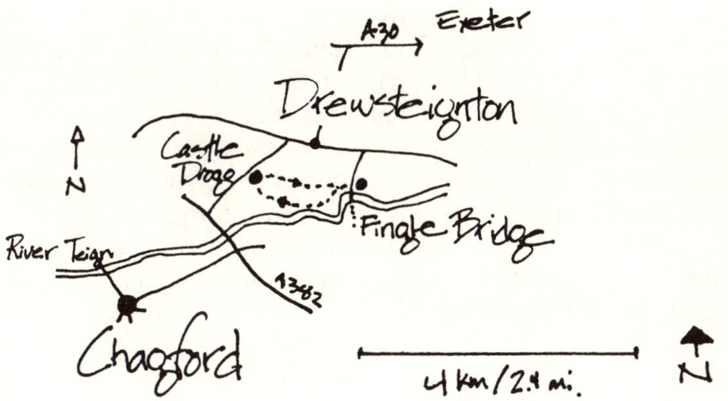

Drive from Chagford to Fingle Bridge—3 miles
Coffee: *Angler's Rest*
Walk from Fingle Bridge to Castle Drogo via Teigne River Trail—2 3/4 miles
Lunch: *Castle Drogo*
Walk from Castle Drogo to Fingle Bridge via the Hunter's trail—2 1/4 miles
Drive to Chagford via Drewsteignton

Today we walked five and a half miles up and down in a countryside completely different from the Cotswolds. We began by browsing in Chagford and toyed with the idea of buying walking sticks. But they were too expensive and we'd rather find our own. We drove to Fingle Bridge and enjoyed coffee outside at Angler's Rest on the banks of the Teigne. Our walk began through the forest by the river where I loved singing, "K-K-K-Katie, Beautiful Katie," and "Wait Till the Sun Shines Nellie." When we didn't see signs for a long time I began my usual worry, "What if we're lost?" I began picking honeysuckle and foxgloves to quiet nagging thoughts. After two miles we finally came upon a sign to Castle Drogo, way up a hill.

At the top were swarms of flies so we dashed into the castle to escape our "enemy." The castle is a national trust house built between 1910 and 1930, massive and ugly, except for wonderful, giant wooden tables, washboards, and drainboards in the kitchen. I was disappointed not to discover a *real old* castle in the land where there are so many; however, we could view the beauty of Dartmoor, gorges, and forests below.

We lunched at the castle and Perry fared better with a pâté than I, with a too fishy sardine sandwich. We began our ramble this time on the hunter's trail, high up among the foxgloves, ferns, bright dandelions, and lots of heather. *But*, the flies were so thick around our heads and bodies that I started screaming at them, until I covered my head with the hood of my jacket and took to swatting them with fern fronds in one hand, and using my large bouquet as a windshield wiper across my face. As we dropped lower into the forest, the flies disappeared and huge colonies of ants took their place. While the latter reminded me of purposeful and rewarding work in my active classroom, the flies, which had buzzed in black swarms like a plague, brought up a desire to kill one of my supervisors who had driven me crazy with constant interruptions. Rambling gives me time to allow murderous impulses to surface so I can chew them over, spit them out, and regain a calmness with which to explore gentler and nonfelonious alternatives to solving problems.

When we returned to Angler's Rest we drove to Drewsteignton, a pretty small town, and then back to Chagford. We talked of moments on this trip when we enjoyed one another's pleasure as much as our own. I was somewhat awestruck that we had come to a place in our lives that we had dreamed of being but somehow never thought we'd reach.

Day 8. From Chagford to Gidleigh Park to Kestor Rock in the Dartmoor Moor to Gidleigh Castle to Gidleigh Park to Chagford.

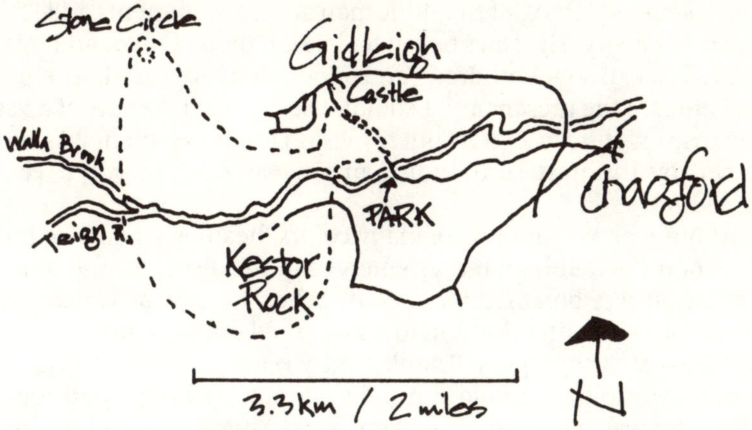

Drive from Chagford to Gidleigh Park—3 miles
Walk from Gidleigh Park to Kestor Rock, and return via Gidleigh Castle—7-8 miles
Lunch: *picnic at Kestor Rock*
Coffee: *Gidleigh Castle*
Drive to Chagford—2 miles

Last night I dreamed of a man who had been so cruel to me in my youth. In my dream he appeared a beggar whom I'd left behind long ago. He appealed to my compassion, which I gave in the form of a nod, a tear, and a look of forgiveness. I couldn't sleep after that. I wonder if the dream occurred because Perry and I had been appreciating the riches we shared together, which allowed me to feel the sadness for those in my family from whom I'd moved away.

Today was a very exciting and awesome day out on the Dartmoor Moor. There is nothing like really walking, *being* on the moors which I've read about, heard about, and seen only in movies. We started walking from Gidleigh Park with an ordnance survey map and a lunch in our backpack, ready for an eight- or nine-mile ramble. We walked along uphill in flowered woods—so long a climb it seemed. Then suddenly, the moor appeared from nowhere—it took my breath away as we walked up and out onto it. Long-haired sheep introduced us to a vast expanse. I became frightened of losing my sense of direction and not trusting Perry's, so we started out holding hands, then walking slightly apart. I was the first to come upon some stones. There's something exciting and terribly eerie about coming across a stone circle similar to Stonehenge, though much smaller. I think of Neolithic man and encampments and I feel a part of history. The skies began to darken, then lighten, and mists poured in quickly, withdrew, and suddenly reappeared. The past had entered the present and I couldn't see beyond. I knew of a vast expanse of future out there, but my vision for the moment was contained by the mist surrounding me. I was relieved when Perry joined me.

At our feet were mosses of many colors, heather, a real peat bog. Piles of rocks and high moors emerged in the distance, and a river not far off. We breathed more easily when we saw a woman and child, and soon after that a man who turned out to be just what we needed—a cartographer. Thank God we found him because our ordnance survey map did not indicate that the bridge had rotted away; he was remapping that very area. After receiving his directions, we climbed high, and as the wind began to blow we hid behind Kestor Rock on a ledge, slightly free of sheep manure. We could eat our lunch there without too much difficulty—until the rain came. Perry was more confident than I in finding a way down without getting lost. We separated a few yards from one another for a while, still keeping within sight as we walked in and out of mists. As we continued our way down, the views were beautiful, and we enjoyed wild ponies, sheep, and sheepherders on horseback. Our Gortex jackets and pants kept us dry and only slightly chilled.

We descended through the forest filled with flowers, passed below the level of black flies and rested at a river where we ate the rest of our lunch, sitting on a space blanket that Perry had carried in his pack. Then on we walked to Gidleigh Castle for coffee. There are remains of a Saxon structure, an 11th-century Norman tower, and a nice spot to sit outside by the ruins. The castle itself has been converted into a not very attractive inn; but we enjoyed listening to its history, told by the proprietor. What an awesome day it was—like discovering one of the wonders of the world.

Trip 2: Colmar, Alsace Region of France

We chose the area around Alsace, with the center in Colmar, because we wanted a change of scenery, culture, custom, and menu. Colmar can be reached by train easily from Paris or Frankfurt, or by rental car from Basle, Switzerland. It is surrounded by beautiful countryside and close to the wonderful towns of Strasbourg, France, and Freiburg, Germany—just across the Rhine.

We rumbled by car from one winery to another, then rambled in charming towns, then into the country in back of wineries on trails into the Vosges mountains. The town of Colmar has so much of what Paris has to offer, but without the crowds and hugeness. Food selections in many miniature groceries are similar to the very fancy Fauchon on the Madeleine in Paris; museums, churches, and half-timbered houses are masterpieces; and we consider the shopping and eating establishments among the finest in the world.

Days 1 and 2. Basle, Switzerland to Colmar, France to Ammerschwihr and back to Colmar.

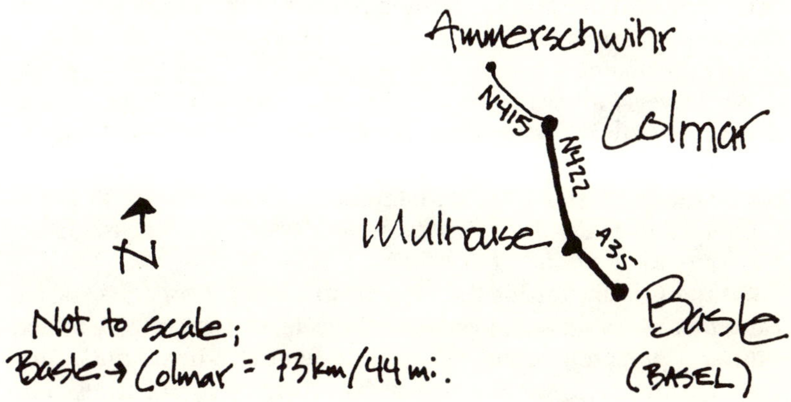

Drive from Basle to Colmar—44 miles (Day 1)
Walk from Hotel Terminus Bristol through Colmar town and return—5.2 miles
Dinner: *Rendez-vous de Chasse, Hotel Terminus Bristol (Day 1)*
Drive to Ammerschwihr—5 miles (Day 2)
Dinner: *Aux Armes de France, Ammerschwihr (Day 2)*
Hotel: *Terminus Bristol, Colmar*

Yesterday was a travel day, always hard because of change. Perry was anxious, with overly high expectations of himself in foreign territory, and I, too, suddenly expected that I SHOULD understand everything, and speak French without error, just because I graduated with honors in French many years ago!

When our flight to Basle became rough I said to myself, "If the plane goes down, please dear God, let it do so quickly so I won't have to feel the pain." I continued to worry, "Have I left my affairs in good enough order at home?" I hated the fleeting thought of my orphan children, though proud to know how well they were doing. At this very good point in my life I have my worst fantasies of disaster. I remembered, finally, to breathe deeply and slowly, letting each breath pass gently around and through my anxiety like comforting hands—until the plane landed safely.

At the Hertz rent-a-car counter Perry's jaw was tense as he rustled through papers, searching frantically for numbers as if he were back in the business world. I don't think he really started breathing with any depth at all until after we almost ended up in a ditch as we were driving away from the airport. Having made a mistake, he then seemed more at ease; though neither of us was able to really calm or comfort the other, at least we didn't turn to deprecating remarks for being anxious.

We drove 44 miles in pouring rain on an autoroute from Basle to Colmar, where we were to stay for three nights at the Terminus Bristol, across from the train depot. The hotel is antique, not fancy, old-fashioned with a wonderful intimate elevator lined in thick upholstery, and a very fine restaurant, Rendez-vous de Chasse, (rated two stars by the Guide Michelin).

Dinner was like tasting the work of an artist. I chose from the à la carte menu—salad and *grenouilles* (frogs legs), which were boned, tiny, and prepared succulently with a light and delightful watercress cream sauce. My dessert was blackberries, strawberries, a little pineapple, and fresh *cassis* (currant) ice. Yum! I was delighted to find it less expensive than Perry's whole dinner; he usually teases me that the à la carte menu is much more expensive. Perry loved his *écrevisses* (crawfish) bisque, a light salmon with hollandaise sauce, a beautifully cooked steak, and Munster cheese of the region. We had two wines and went to bed feeling as delicious as what we had seen, smelled, and tasted.

At 9:30 this morning we set out on foot, without rain but under very cloudy skies, to the Unterlinden Museum in the main part of town. We'd just begun to be disappointed on our walk from the hotel with nothing of much interest, until suddenly the sights became more and more fascinating. The butcher shops, cheese, fruit, and vegetable stands had magnificent produce set in artistic displays. The wine shops were filled with *eau de vie* (translated as "water of life"—or essence) of pear, raspberry, and myrtleberry.

The bakeries were filled with meringues in the shape of birds with beaks made of almonds. I bought a few green almonds, two sweet white peaches, a small bottle of *eau de vie de poire* (pear essence), a goat cheese, and felt in heaven.

In a downpour of rain we arrived at the Unterlinden Museum, surrounded by wonderful 13th- to 15th-century half-timbered houses. Inside the museum, the alterpiece was most exciting—the best monsters I've ever seen—some with great eagle beaks ripping into human victims with red and green oozing sores. What phenomena were these artists of the Middle Ages trying to explain? Were they trying to externalize what was going on inside of them? Were they trying to purge themselves of their devils who robbed them of the good things in life? How fascinating is the concept of the good and evil characters within each one of us in our own inner theater! Perry left me to my thoughts while he continued to see more paintings.

As the rain let up, we put our Gortex pants in our backpack and set out to the Dominican church, with the Vierge Buisson and some fine 15th-century windows. The cathedral was under construction and we decided to take a break for lunch. One after another patisseries were filled, and I grew impatient, not realizing that if we wanted lunch without waiting we'd have to start by 12:00. In France, everything closes at 12:30 for two hours. Again I wanted to eat in the park, but gave my decision to Perry who chose a restaurant where we only had to wait a little while. I left to go to the restroom before the waiter came to take our order, having first rehearsed with Perry what he could say to the waiter and how to point to the items we wanted to order. When I returned Perry was triumphant. For the first time he had given the order in French. We seemed to plow through many courses, and just as Perry was about to ask for the bill, the chef proudly poked his head out of the kitchen onto the courtyard where we were sitting, and the waiter appeared with a large fish.

"What the hell happened? What did you say?" I questioned. Perry, very perplexed, said, "Let's see. I pointed to the things on the menu and then I said, 'et du poisson' because there were two of us." "You said WHAT? Oh my God! Two people is not 'du poisson', that means 'some fish.' Two people is 'deux personnes'." With the waiter at the table, we held hands tightly under the table and kept our mouths closed. We were both too shy to tell either waiter or cook that we'd made a mistake; besides, the cook would have seen us if we'd dumped it. Somehow we mooshed the fish around the plate, and snuck some of it into our napkins. Language errors are at once an extreme frustration, a challenge, and a source of great laughter.

At 2:00 the town became alive again, and we enjoyed strolling in and out of shops, tasted wine, and bought some apricots. My French is both better and worse than I expected. Sometimes I surprise myself and other times search wildly for a word I think I ought to remember. As we sat for a coffee, we talked about how France is so colorful, artistic, delicious, and tasteful; yet somehow it is also cold and impersonal, with stultifying rules left over from another era. What a paradox!

We rested before dinner and then drove to a fine restaurant outside of town in Ammerschwihr. I could hardly eat after lunch but Perry was raring to go again. He was uncomfortable about speaking French, feels like a second-class citizen because of his inadequacy in a foreign language. I emphasized he was a first-class citizen as far as I was concerned, and just because he came to France where he's unaccustomed to manners and language did not make him a second-class citizen—just an uncomfortable first-class one. Then we laughed and began to flirt, shared our journals, and I got somewhat tipsy because I hadn't watched how much wine I'd tasted, nor how much *eau de vie de Gewurtztraminer* (wine essence with high alcoholic content) sherbet I slurped. I sang French songs learned in childhood all the way back to Colmar, and we got to bed later than we had in ages—12:15, a record.

Day 3. Colmar to Sigolsheim to Kaysersberg to Kientzheim to Bennwihr and Mittelwihr, then to Riquewihr to Hunawihr to Ribeauvillé to Colmar.

Drive to Sigolsheim—3 miles
Drive to Kaysersberg—3.9 miles
Walk into the forest of the Vosges Mountains in back of Kaysersberg, loop trip—3 miles
Lunch: *café in Kaysersberg*
Drive to Kientzheim—2 miles
Drive through Bennwihr, Mittelwihr to Riquewihr—4.3 miles
Ice Cream: *Riquewihr*
Drive to Hunawihr and Ribeauvillé—2.8 miles
Tea: *café in Ribeauvillé*
Drive to Colmar—10 miles
Dinner: *Maison des Têtes, Colmar*

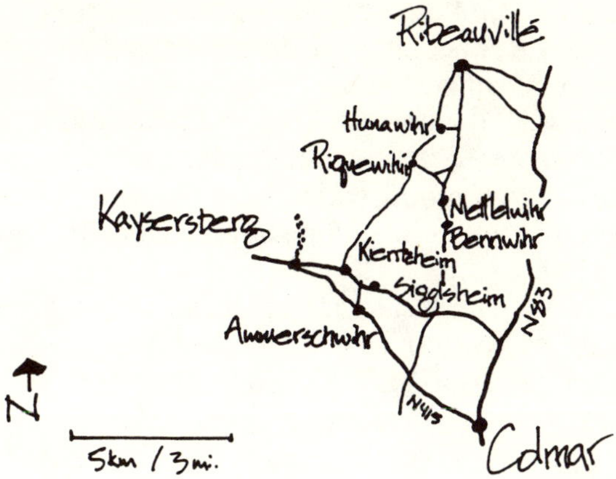

Today I awoke with a familiar feeling I hadn't experienced in many years—grainy throat, sand in the eyes, slight nausea, and a remembrance of a taste from the night before. A slight hangover from wine and sherbet, of all things.

We'd bought a map of the region yesterday, and looked forward to the countryside. After breakfast we rumbled off to Sigolsheim where we enjoyed the view from the top of the town, over green vineyards—so tidy, clipped, and perfectly manicured. The houses appeared almost polished clean, brownish-red in color, with window boxes everywhere filled with red and pink geraniums. When we arrived in Kaysersberg we parked and walked through the town streets, and chose a trail up into the mountains in back of town—steep into the forest. The view was magnificent overlooking vineyards and houses. I picked a bouquet of dark pinks, thyme, wild phlox, and yellow campanulas, and needed to stop often because of my "sherbet hangover." Perry stumbled, blamed his eyesight on older age. "Tired," I responded, "just plain old tired"—not wanting to talk about aging at the moment. Besides I wasn't sure; can't a person stumble at any age, especially if he or she is overextended?

We walked back to town by way of the 12th-century castle, standing in ruins. Rain spattered just as we reached a lovely little café for omelette and salad by 12:15. We poked into shops, and drove a bit to Kientzheim, where a wine fête was just finishing. Countryside continued beautiful on the route to Bennwihr, Mittelwihr, and Riquewihr, a town on the opposite side of the mountain where we'd rambled in the morning. Riquewihr is a beautiful town, with too many tourists and an overpowering number of

16th-century half-timbered houses, courtyards, wine cellars, and souvenir shops. I had an apricot ice before rumbling on to Hunawihr which had everything to commend it without souvenir shops or tourists. We moseyed along on back roads through vineyards to Ribeauvillé, a nontourist, working people's town with a lovely hotel of seven rooms where we'd like to stay. After tea we decided to return to Colmar for sleeping, reading, and healing time.

Dinner at a one-star restaurant in a beautiful, old building, the Maison des Têtes, was not as good as we'd hoped, although I did like my *truite bleu* (trout) and chicken on the less expensive menu than Perry's larger, more expensive, and greasier dinner. We talked about how much we enjoyed spending time together on this trip and recalled the many, many dinners at home spent in asking one another what we liked and didn't like about one another's behaviors, followed by discussions about what each of us was willing or not willing to change. How much we cared.

Trip 3: Lienz in the Osttirol, Austria

We chose Lienz, Austria, for the center of our rambles—on the spur of the moment in the middle of a trip to Sporz (in the Grison area of Switzerland), Merano (in the Italian Tyrol), Asolo (a town of Palladian villas an hour's drive from Venice), the Gardena Pass area in the Italian Dolomites, and Vaduz (the hub of rambling in Lichtenstein).

We had arrived in Asolo during a giant wave of heat and tourists, and decided to abort our plans in and around Venice, choosing instead the cooler mountains. Lienz, from photographs in the *Relais et Chateaux* guide, looked like a charming town, had good hotel recommendations, and was in beautiful rambling and camping country near the Grossglöckner Pass. We would not be far from the next spot on our itinerary, in the Dolomite country where we were meeting friends for a few days of rambling.

Day 1. From Asolo via Cortina, Italy to Lienz, Austria.

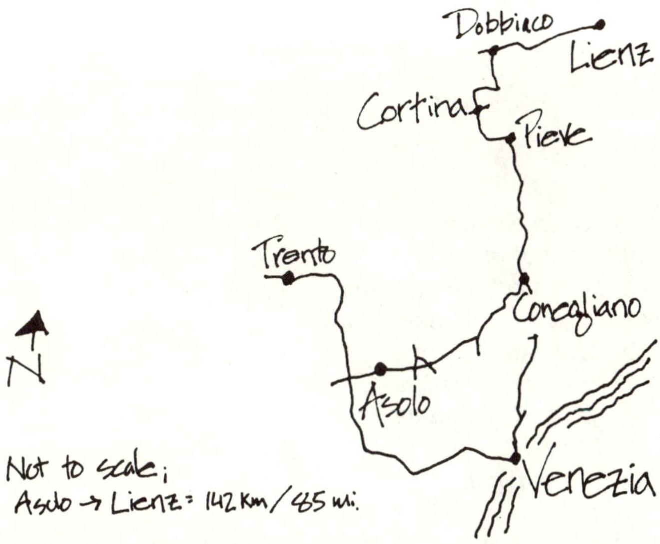

Drive to Cortina—85 miles
Lunch: *Hotel de la Poste, Cortina*
Drive to Lienz—48 miles
Dinner: *Hotel Traube, Lienz*
Hotel: *Hotel Traube*

Day 2. From Lienz to Schlossbrück to Sternalm to Moos Alm House to Gribelehof Pension to Lienz.

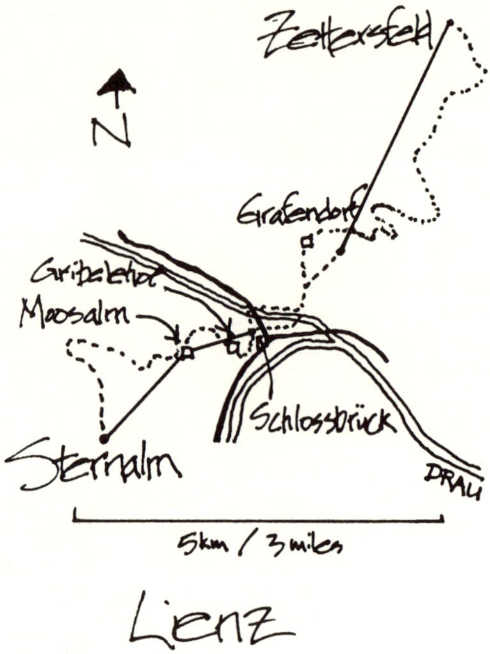

Walk to Schloss Sesselift *(chairlift)—2 miles*
Sesselift to top of mountain
Coffee: *Sternalm Mountain Inn*
Walk to Moos Alm House—3 miles
Lunch: *Moos Alm House*
Walk to Gribelehof Pension—2 miles
Drinks: *Gribelehof Pension*
Walk to Lienz—2 miles
Dinner: *Hotel Traube*

Yesterday we took a four and a half hour—85 mile long, hot, winding drive through the Dolomites from Asolo to Lienz, stopping in Cortina for lunch. The heat destroys our perspective on everything. We'd expected to stay four more days in and around Venice but instead took only a day-trip to satisfy Perry's desire to visit that romantic city. The light overlooking the canal was pure white in the waves of heat. Tourists covered the Piazza San Marco like an army of ants, their noses scrunched up as they looked up at decorated wedding-cake buildings that appeared to be melting into the water. Thousands fanned themselves in outdoor cafés while a stale perspiration odor lingered in our nostrils. I was in unspeakable humor, terrible looking, with hair limp and tousled, and pale face as we sat down for apricot-and-lemon ice. Perry, too, was speechless, exhausted, his face blotchy. At that moment nothing that was "supposed to be pleasurable" gave any pleasure at all. We'd stopped trying to be good sports. How difficult it was to accept our disappointment in spending so much money and not enjoying a special place acclaimed as a wondrous historic and artistic city. We had meant it to be wonderful for us too. But it lost its appeal because of our discomfort. No sight seemed worth this price.

How relieved we were to leave the heat of Italy and be flexible enough to change our plans. Our room in the Hotel Traube overlooks the shops and the river, with a view of the mountains. While Perry collapsed on the bed, I decided to go swimming in the indoor pool on the roof. After reading a rule for wearing bathing caps, I stubbornly refused to buy one, so designed a makeshift one from a plastic bag imprinted with a Cutty Sark label, and tied it to my head with Perry's rubber clothes line. I nodded as politely as possible to an elderly English couple stepping into the pool with me. I usually hate the smell of over-chlorination in indoor pools as well as the feeling of being closed in, somewhat like Alice in Wonderland in a dark pool of tears. However, this pool was better than most, perhaps because I needed to cool off. "Is my extreme discomfort with the heat a symptom of older age?" I wondered. If so, I was willing to accept it as a limitation and choose cooler climates whenever possible.

Today we were both in good humor at breakfast, and enjoyed eating a very hard and chewy rye bread pronounced something like "finch-go-lo-bel," along with fruit, cheese, liverwurst, and café-au-lait. Perry liked conversing with a lady desk clerk who suntans herself on the roof garden, and who gave us directions for our rambles today. First, we walked along the wooded promenade by the river for two miles to the Schloss *sesselift* (chairlift). Arriving at the top, we enjoyed a short walk through magnificent stands of lupine to Sternalm, a mountain inn where we had mineral water and discussed whether or not it was a good idea to walk all the way down from the top. If not, we could take the *sesselift* back to the first station. How wonderful it is in Switzerland and Austria that we ramblers, unlike trekkers, can take as long or as short a walk as our physical limitations will allow. We decided we could ramble all the way and I sang lustily—every song I ever knew—for three steep miles down, occasionally stopping to pick blueberries along the way.

After an hour and a half we stopped for lunch at Moos Alm House, where Perry somehow ordered a kind of awful spam with a hard fried egg on top, accompanied by potatoes and wine. I fared better with frankfurter and bread, so I ordered another for Perry which helped him survive, he said later. Then down, down, down we walked to the Gribelehof Pension, our way marked by several crucifixes to the side of benches tucked in the woods on beautiful footpaths lined with flowers and ferns. At the Gribelehof Pension we drank iced mineral water with lemon. I began to worry about my back because going downhill for eight miles is a strain. I was thankful, however, that my legs no longer ached as they had when we began our first downhill rambles in Switzerland two weeks earlier. It takes time to build up our muscles these days.

We arrived back at the hotel by 5:00, swam, rested, and ate dinner outside under an awning. I couldn't understand the menu in German and was concentrating so hard on choosing food that I did comprehend, that I wasn't paying attention to the waiter who was explaining in English. As a result of not listening, I wound up with too much pasta.

The temperature was perfect and we enjoyed the evening air and feeling unpressured as we people-watched. British tourists were enjoying the same activity, demonstrated by polite whispers and a few giggles behind hands held to their mouths. Children were playing giant checkers and chess in the street across the way.

After dinner, an Austrian band marched along the street, and we joined the throng of followers. Such fun.

Day 3. From Lienz to Zettersfeld funicular to the top of the Zettersfeld to Grafendorf Herdenhof to Lienz.

Walk to the Zettersfeld funicular—1 mile
Funicular to the top of Zettersfeld
Walk to the café near the top of the mountain—1/4-1/2 mile
Snack: *café near the top of the mountain*
Walk to Grafendorf Herdenhof Pension—8 miles
Ice Cream: *Grafendorf Herdenhof*
Walk to Lienz—1 mile
Dinner: *Hotel Traube*

We broke our record today by walking ten and a half miles, eight of which were steeply downhill. Not a great idea; we learned a lesson. Not *all* mountains have inns to stop midway for lunch. It's best to check *before* boarding a chairlift or tram. Also, just because a funicular or tram takes no time to go up, it doesn't mean that the way down is fast or easy.

We began walking across the town of Lienz to the Zettersfeld funicular which zoomed to the top of the mountain. Perry found a sign indicating "3 std. route #5," meaning a three-hour walk. "For the *average* hiker," I said, and we're *not*—we're *much* slower. Undaunted, Perry announced we were inveterate hikers by now and although the automobiles below seemed like tiny ants, I somehow believed Perry, or thought I *should*! We stopped at the only café near the top, and not understanding the menu, I wound up with an awful sausage dripping with fat, and Perry tried to order what he thought was thin dried beef or ham, but instead got "speck"—a ham with giant layers of fat.

The first part of the walk was beautiful but steep, a logging trail, then a paved road with switchbacks for mile after mile. We enjoyed vistas of valleys, river, and the spectacular Dolomites as a backdrop; however, my feet, knee joints, and hips felt stiff. Perry fell in a hole, lagged behind and didn't let me know why, while I grew fearful, no longer trusting my body with confidence. I began to develop twinges of pain in my lower back, and in panic, heard terrible voices inside my head with cruel judgement, hammering: "Margot, shame on you! You're not a good sport, not a fit specimen after all. Fine model of caretaking *you* are. You *should* have known the trail was that steep and long. Now you're going to ruin this trip for Perry. You'll have to stay here, stuck, maybe till nightfall, while Perry will have to go miles to get help." I lay down in the middle of the path and practiced breathing exercises to relax my muscles, while I remembered my sister who had been so supportive of me two years ago when I'd injured my back. She'd listened to my deprecating voices and talked with me in such a caring way, so that when I was ready to continue walking, I was determined to use my memory of her voice. Without upsetting myself further, I stood up slowly and for the remainder of the long journey I used what I recalled, "One step at a time, Margot. See! That was a good one! You're breathing fine now. Look how far you've come!"

At last, four hours later, we arrived at Grafendorf Herdenhof Pension for *eis kaffee* (coffee over vanilla ice cream), and hobbled back to the hotel to sleep for a long time. At dinner we chatted with a couple from Manchester, England, enjoyed hearing about their daily lives and travels, and then observed a couple about whom Perry reported: "They talk to one another like sea urchins." And he was right; their mouths were held tightly in the shape of round holes, only their teeth moved to do the talking. What a relief it was to laugh tonight.

Day 4. From Lienz to Heiligenblüt on the Grossglöckner Pass (Hochalpenstrasse) on the Franz Josef Highway to Lienz.

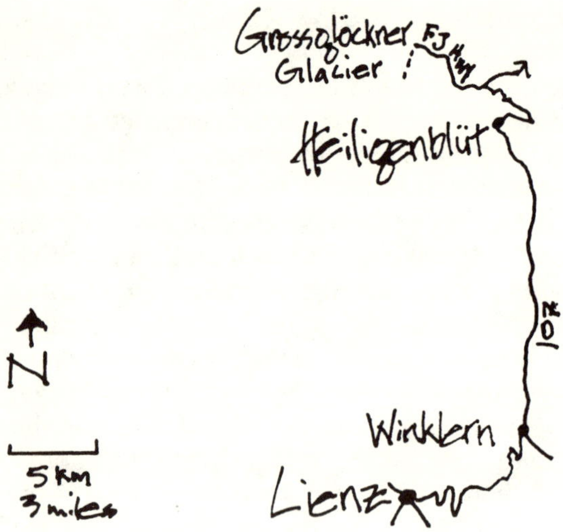

Drive to Heiligenblüt—23.8 miles
Drive to Hochalpenstrasse to Grossglöckner Glacier on the Franz Josef Highway—16 miles
Cable Car to the Glacier
Drive to Lienz—39.8 miles
Dinner: *Hotel Traube*

After two days of more hiking than we're used to (yesterday was far more than rambling), and a healthy fear of injury, we took a short drive today, up the Grossglöckner Pass to Heiligenblüt, where we stopped at a church recommended by the hotel desk clerk. We continued along the twisty road, with more than forty well-banked turns and a profusion of wild flowers; my favorite was wild eidelweiss, which only grows in high alpine country. The top of the

Grossglöckner Pass (Hochalpenstrasse) was freezing cold as we found ourselves enveloped in a cloud. After parking the car and avoiding most of the tourists crowding into unattractive souvenir shop-restaurants, we took a cable car down close to the glacier—terribly blowy, cold, and scary. Rocks and debris from the earth had collected to form a black surface over the ice, with eerie blue crevices underneath. The path of a glacier is awesome, like a giant frozen lava flow. How close seemed fire and ice. We stood for a while, shivering.

We could have proceeded on a full-day drive as we'd wanted—to Eidelweiss Pass, over and down to Ferleiten Wildlife Park, to Brück, the Zeller See, Mittersill, and back to Lienz through the Felbertauerntunnel; however, we chose to stroll leisurely, paint, and read today. I especially loved *The Professor's House* by Willa Cather. Her descriptions of the Southwest United States reminded me of the Jemez mountains there, near Santa Fe—so different from here. I felt the colors of the earth there like clay pots I'd held in my hands, and then saw those colors rising to meet the blue sky until all became one. I find a balance there, like on a horizon line tightrope between earth and sky, day and night, heavy and light, negative and positive space.

Tonight I felt like Cather's professor, as he moved into older age—enjoying his memories going back to boyhood, yet worrying about "doing nothing." I want time to just stare into space, do nothing; I worry about maybe never wanting to do anything again. Perhaps just the opposite is true—my most creative years are yet to come. The thought comforts me.

Day 5. From Lienz to Leisach to Bannberg to Bannberger Alm toward Bösem Weibele to Bannberger Alm to Lienz.

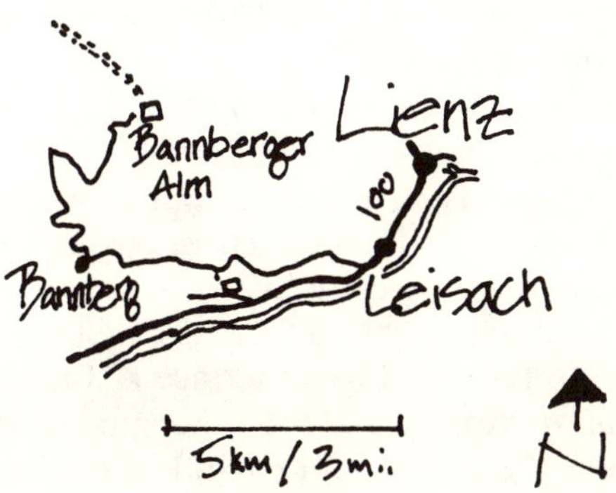

Drive to Bannberger Alm via Leisach and Bannberg—10 miles
Walk toward Bösem Weibele and return to Bannberger Alm—3 1/2 miles
Lunch: *Bannberger Alm*
Drive to Lienz—10 miles
Dinner: *Hotel Traube*

Today was just right—weather truly magnificent, no clouds, not too hot—and we rambled on an unexpected "best walk of all." Perry classifies it as one of the tops in the world.

This morning I hid behind a post in the lobby, waiting for the desk clerk I trusted to come out from the office. (A bitchy second clerk had given another couple second-class advice I'd noted while eavesdropping yesterday). When "my" clerk appeared I dashed for the desk and asked her to recommend a favorite walk. We drove a short distance just past Leisach, where we turned right, went up and up to about 2100 meters to the tiny town of Bannberg, then to the end of the road—Bannberger Alm—where we parked the car by a lovely grassy terrace in the sun with umbrellas.

We rambled toward Bösem Weibele, along a ridge high up, with valleys on either side, the Dolomites so clearly sculptured—one side belonging to Italy and the other to Austria. We walked for an hour through fields of flowers and I was in ecstasy just smelling the earth—my whole being ringing alive, excited like a child. This was a special moment after years of hard work in our personal and professional lives. I felt Perry's stubby fingers and weathered hands which he'd always complained were "old hands" even when he was young and working on his grandfather's rice ranch. I loved holding his hand and smoothing it, loving him for his touch with the earth, the solid ground, the rational and sensible, as well as the sensitive. In smoothing his hand I ran over rough places, skin cancers, which sometimes scared him. Touching him today somehow helped me to understand him.

On a carpet of blues, pinks, lavenders, whites, and yellows, we spread out our space blanket, feeling on top of the world, in the warm sun, under blue sky, and holding yet another new flower—a tiny greenish-white orchid. After retracing our path, we looked across the mountains where we had hiked two days before, and stopped for a most reasonably priced lunch of trout, salad, potatoes, and wine on the uncrowded terrace of Bannberger Alm.

Back in Lienz we strolled, and to my delight Perry found an Austrian jacket; I love the way he looks in it. He bought me a lovely pot of growing edelweiss and I was touched. The day was perfect and we both knew it. I wondered aloud if awful days are produced so that we appreciate the beautiful ones? How terrible it would be to have beautiful days on the outside and feel miserably depressed inside. It's wonderful when both outside and inside match. Perry looked at me and in a soft voice said, "Margot, write that down and circle it. That's good!"

What is your response to these types of rambling trips?

If you choose to ramble, where would you go?

What needs, desires, and limitations would you need to consider?

If you kept a journal what would you like to write about?

5

On the Trip

The two of you can use this chapter either to evaluate one of your earlier trips before planning a new one or to guide you while on the special trip you've just planned.

PROBLEMS ON THE FIRST LEG OF THE TRIP

Strategies you've devised for resolving problems before leaving home won't always work out as expected. You may need to experiment with a technique for a longer time than you had originally planned before obtaining desired results, or you may need to drop the strategy and find an alternative.

How Do Your Strategies Work Out?

About to embark upon a carefully planned month-long trip, Perry was excited about leaving. He had worked hard and was satisfied that he had done all he could to take care of last-minute details at the office and at home. He was quite relaxed while my anxieties were worse than usual, though I, too, had planned carefully. I'd made a list of all the things I'd done in preparation, which included sharing my worries with family and friends, then writing down each concern on separate pieces of paper and placing them in a box for safekeeping so they wouldn't come along to bother me on our trip. I managed to say I'd allow three worries to accompany me on the plane so I would avoid perfectionism. Friends and family had written notes in a book to remind me of something special I meant to them. I took along three tape recordings: a heart-warming conversation among friends, a soft voice offering directions for breathing and relaxation, and favorite selections of music.

But I still felt grumbly and slightly apprehensive. So, I took out my journal on the plane and wrote:

> How I hate going away right at this time when Mark and Karen are going to share news of having a baby. We're going to be grandparents for the first time!

"The world should stop over this news," I thought, and while feeling even more annoyed, I continued to write of an immediate aggravation:

> I can't stand the smell of cigarettes and air-conditioning. I've been thrown out into the world beyond and I don't want to be.

And then I thought:

> This writing is not helping, not at all. Well, I'll try one or two more worries.

I wrote of our children's problems and that I'd like to find a way to help them respect their differences. Still grousing that I wasn't feeling better, I took to writing down the menu and trying to guess what the fancy French words really meant. My favorite translated as "dog food smothered with wine outside a casserole." At least I was progressing to humor, and almost ready to listen to one of my tapes. I looked out the window:

> As we go further north it's lighter. The sun is orange—setting on black clouds. The moon is the thinnest of crescents. How wonderful to come from dark into light. It's a fine, fine line—like the one that leads from the end of my breath to the beginning of a new one.

I continued:

> I long to see and feel colors on this trip—the pinks I'd remembered in the columbine with the yellow centers to be discovered all over again. And the pinks in Fra Angelico's paintings.

I found myself unexpectedly immersed in my travels with a clear direction, after riding out my worries and frustrations and adventures of the moment through writing. My fellow travelers (those not peacefully sleeping) were reading, writing, listening to tapes, playing cards, knitting, playing word games, or chatting. And I wondered how they might be using these activities as strategies to avoid or take care of their worries.

What difficulties did you anticipate before leaving home?

How did you handle whatever difficulties arose?

If your strategies did not work out as you had expected, did you:

1. **drop the strategy and find an alternative?**
2. **give up with a sense of defeat, frustration, disappointment, anger?**
3. **count the experience in your allowance for mistakes?**
4. **learn something that you could apply at another time?**

How Do You Deal With Mishaps?

Sometimes, even when you anticipate difficulties before leaving home and take precautions to eliminate a problem, you still cannot predict or prevent mishaps. How you handle the experience and what you learn from it make the difference between coming out on the bottom of the heap with disappointment and resentment, and coming out on the top with pride in taking on a challenge and doing what you can.

My mother had changed from the Woman-of-Tantrums, a victim in the Calcutta airport, into an artful traveler. Before her last trip from San Francisco to Rome, she focused her attention on packing lightly (in case she might not find a sky cap or baggage cart) and putting her essential medicines, toilet articles, important papers, and a clean blouse in an overnight bag. She also decided to break up the long flight by stopping overnight in New York, near the airport.

Thus forewarned and forearmed, she arrived at the San Francisco airport and smilingly beckoned a sky cap. He returned her smile, looked at her ticket, and said, "So, you're off to Rome!" "Yes," she nodded, "but not today—tomorrow." She watched him affix the tags to her baggage and carefully placed her receipts inside her ticket envelope. Satisfied that she had taken care of all that needed to be cared for, she enjoyed her flight to Kennedy airport. But after landing she waited—and waited—and waited at the baggage carousel. An hour later, her bag had still not arrived. Off she went to Lost and Found, where she met another woman with a similar problem. But she'd lost her temper along with her bags and was complaining hysterically about the perils of travel, the incompetence of airline personnel, and the unmitigated evil of the universe. The woman's carrying on reinforced my mother's determination to stay calm. A glance at her overnight bag, with everything she really needed for two days, reassured her.

What had happened? She thought she had checked *everything*. The clerk at Lost and Found examined her ticket, which read San Francisco—New York, New York—Rome, and her baggage tag, which read FCO. Ah, her suitcase had been routed straight to FCO, Fiumicino, the airport outside Rome.

Suddenly she knew what had happened. In her moment of flirtation and gratitude at having found a sky cap she had neglected to read the tag. Hurdles. But she was winning. She asked the clerk to call Rome to hold her suitcase, lest someone there do her the favor of returning it to New York. For further reassurance she later phoned the airline herself from her motel room. She fantasied the worst that might happen—that her carefully packed suitcase would be lost forever. "Good," she exclaimed, "then I'll go buy all new clothes and send TWA the bill. What's better than Rome for a new wardrobe? Damn, though. I don't want to spend my time that way, and I *don't* want to hassle with the paperwork."

The next day her bag was waiting for her in Rome. That night she celebrated her threefold success: her new-found calmness in handling a mishap, her planning for an overnight bag in case of emergency, and her thinking of alternatives had her bag been lost permanently. To her mental list of preparations for future trips she added:

- Ask the sky cap or ticket agent to translate the code on the luggage tags.
- Check that the code on the tag matches the point of arrival on the ticket.
- Make sure the boarding agent tears the correct sheet from the ticket packet.

A favorite story of mine about responding creatively to mishaps is my friend Paul's tale of flying from San Francisco to Salt Lake City—in only twelve hours. He'd offered to take Megan's skis and luggage along with his own on a Friday evening flight, meet her flight on Saturday, and enjoy a weekend of skiing. Megan arrived with no difficulty but Paul did not appear until two hours later, somewhat the worse for wear, but with a slight smile indicating he'd met his match and won a victory.

Paul's flight had left San Francisco on time Friday night, but the Salt Lake airport had been socked in by fog. After circling for two and a half hours, the pilot received word to go on to Boise. At Boise, a long line of passengers quickly formed to ask for assistance—if they couldn't continue to Salt Lake that night, then how would they get there in the morning? If they had to spend the night at a motel would the airlines pay for expenses, and if so, where would they recommend staying?

Paul surveyed the line of panicky people making no forward movement and reasoned quickly. First and foremost he needed to rest in order to regain his humor and his energy. (He already was cursing his gallantry or foolishness in having offered to bring all the skis and baggage and lug them around by himself.) If necessary he would risk paying some of his expenses to avoid all the hassle if the airlines refused.

So he turned away from the crowd, darted into a phone booth, and flipped the yellow pages in search of a motel with a AAA rating. He phoned for a reservation, figuring that rooms would be hard to come by. (He discovered later that his prediction was accurate).

Once at the motel he immediately phoned the airline and was told that passengers were being offered a choice: a bus ride to Salt Lake City or a plane ticket the next day. The bus was to depart at 3:00 a.m. and arrive at 11:00 a.m.; the plane ticket was for Salt Lake via Denver or Seattle, arriving late in the afternoon. The airline maintained that its only responsibility was to "get our people to their destination in the best way we can." Paul reasoned out the consequences and decided he could afford to risk his losses. He immediately phoned another airline and made a reservation on a direct flight the next morning.

As it turned out, the first airline paid for Paul's motel, no meals, and all but $50 of his plane fare from Boise to Salt Lake. Though not everyone can take the gamble, it is important to explore all possibilities for making the best of a bad situation. Paul cautions:

> Airlines no longer coddle you. They change their policies frequently when passengers are stranded so that whatever trick you learn during one trip does not necessarily apply to the next. Be prepared to make changes often, as the airlines do.

If mishaps occurred on the first leg of your trip how did you handle them?

If you reverted to old behaviors what did you learn?

If you used new techniques how were they useful or not useful?

How did you and your partner help to relieve or contribute to one another's anxieties?

What Do You Do in Near Disasters?

Near disasters are rare, but they can happen anywhere, and to avoid acting like a Hysterical Harry or Harriet is a real challenge. Some travelers can deny their fear, but the rest of us Fearing Folk try to knock ourselves out with sleeping pills or tranquilizers, count sheep, chew gum, do needle-point or knit, write or pray. M and M lovers can focus on how long each chocolate takes to dissolve on their tongues, while nail biters have a heyday, and readers pass twenty minutes reading the same line thirty-five times over without comprehension.

There's no way to really prepare for a near disaster—a plane dropping an engine, a tire blowing out at high speeds, a violent storm—but if this happened and you lived to tell the tale you may have learned something valuable about yourselves.

UPON ARRIVAL AT YOUR DESTINATION

Now you and your partner have arrived.

Are you victorious, having met challenges with your skills in using alternatives?

Did the trip work out more smoothly than you had expected? Or do you feel light-headed, with cotton in your mind, tired, flat, disorganized, and wobbly in new surroundings?

Jet Lag

While few travelers seem to have no difficulty crossing time zones, many suffer from jet lag. Others insist that all is well when it really isn't, because they want to "get going" once they have arrived. Deniers disregard their inner time clocks, which tell them to take it easy, and insist on ploughing ahead—irritable, pushy, demanding, unable to rest for the first three days. They often make disparaging remarks to their partners who admit a lack of energy and need for sleep.

Assiduous Avoiders of Jet Lag swear by their elaborate preventive methods. They calculate the number of hours they'll be gaining or losing across time zones and start special diets a few days before leaving home. They even begin changing their routine at home by going to bed one hour later than usual each night for a week in order to adapt more easily to the time zone of their final destination. They choose particular flights and seats, bring their own food, take neither drugs nor alcohol, wear loose-fitting, stain-resistant clothes, practice deep breathing, perform calisthenics in their seats, and learn to jog in place. Once they arrive at their destination they do not go to bed until the local inhabitants do, even though they have not slept for many hours. As a result, they say they are ready to go the next day, good as new.[1]

1. Don Kowet, *The Jet Lag Book,* (New York: Crown Publishers, 1983).

Their repertoire of advice includes:

- Eat spinach four times a day for three days before departure. *Never* eat fatty foods, such as pork—*never.*
- *Never* wear pants that pinch.
- Order special salad on the flight, *never* eat that stuff that tastes like cardboard.
- *Always* wear eye shades and never view the movie.
- Drink a glass of water every half hour on the flight.
- *Never* drink alcohol (because it dehydrates you); *always* bring along a nasal mist.
- Eat very lightly on daytime flights and nothing at all at night.
- Request seats by the bulkhead, grab 3 or 4 blankets, lay them on the floor to cut out the cold air, and take a long snooze.
- Obtain a prescription for sleeping pills.
- Fly first-class: the seats are larger, the cabin more spacious, the air circulation better.

For our next trip I would like to try out the latest method I've heard about from Dr. Michael Finegold, who has developed a self-hypnosis technique for use at one- to two-hour intervals during the flight.[2] Travelers are instructed to close their eyes, use directions to focus on their breathing, and visualize their biological clock. For instance, if it is 1:00 p.m. at home and 9:00 p.m. at your destination, picture yourself at 9:00 p.m. in Europe; two hours later imagine yourself at 11:00 p.m.; and so on throughout the trip. If you consciously become involved in this positive process of changing your biological time, when you land your body rhythm will be more in tune with the new time, and you'll feel more acclimated than if you had kept on thinking, "What would we be doing back at home right now?"

If you're not willing to relinquish meals, wine, or champagne because they contribute to your sense of celebration, you need to decide if they are worth the possible price of jet lag. Perry and I have not tested whether poking around the food and drinking two or three glasses of wine or champagne contribute to our suffering light-headedness for two or three days after we land. We nap immediately for a few hours upon arrival, then go strolling and have a light snack. Perry sleeps well the first night whereas I do not; I'm lucky if I regain my normal sleeping pattern within three nights.

2. Interview with Dr. Michael Finegold, University of California Medical Center, San Francisco, August 22, 1985.

We both function better going east than west, but that may be due to how good a vacation we've had, how much has happened, and how resistant we are to resuming our daily lives at home and work.

What measures have you taken to combat jet lag? Which techniques were useful and which seemed more trouble than they were worth?

If you took no measure to combat jet lag, what were the results?

Are you now interested in trying various measures?

If this is your first long trip, what would you like to do to prevent jet lag?

ENJOYING THE FRUITS OF YOUR LABOR

One of the benefits of planning with some flexibility is that travelers can take advantage of wonderful opportunities that present themselves spontaneously. For example, Ben and Kitty had arranged their last day in London, a visit to the Chelsea Flower Show early in the morning, then on to the Tate Gallery. But Ben found his shoes so filthy from sloshing in the mud at the show grounds that he decided to return to their hotel to change.

The concierge greeted them, took them aside, and whispered, "The manager was just given two tickets which he'd like to offer two guests—to attend the Queen's Presentation of New Colours to the First and Second Battalions of the Cold Stream Guards." Ben looked nonplussed. "I don't know," he replied, "what's that?" The concierge was patient. "It's a very big 'do', happens once in a blue moon. Very important English tradition, you know." Ben and Kitty consulted with one another and accepted. The concierge earnestly replied, "You'll have to be in your seats in half an hour for sure, can't be late. It's a great honor, no more than a thousand invitations are issued." He gave directions and disappeared. Ben and Kitty stared at the invitation. "Morning dress," read Ben. "Good," answered Kitty, "you are wearing clothes for the morning; it *is* morning. Me too, I wear these *every* morning," knowing full well the invitation meant formal morning attire. They edged toward the concierge once again, pointed to "morning dress" and then to themselves, and were reassured they would pass.

Walking quickly toward Whitehall and the Queen's Horse Parade grounds, they came upon road blocks, passed through, and found themselves suddenly among British gentlemen in tall gray Ascot toppers and morning coats; one even wore a monocle. Ben noted moth holes in some of the coats, which had, no doubt, been passed down for many generations—a mark of status or a disguise for their inability to afford new ones. Ladies were dressed as in British films of garden party scenes, with straw hats, feathers and flowers, and yards of chiffon.

The band approached. Kitty grew excited as a child when she realized she could touch the beaver fur on the guard's hat. Detained by a security guard line, they were afraid they wouldn't get to their seats on time after all. Finally they were admitted, and discovered with embarrassment they'd been led to the wrong seats and had to move during the one-step slow march to "Auld Lang Syne." At last as they settled in their right seats, with the band playing and guards marching, *the Queen* arrived in her horse-drawn carriage. What a thrill! After "God Save the Queen," she walked slowly out onto the parade ground, presented the new colors, and as she began a speech, the audience hushed. Suddenly out of St. James Park flew a goose, which circled over the Queen's head, squawked "Blah, blah, blah" as she spoke, then back into the park. Kitty tried to contain her giggle. Such an age-old pageantry that satisfied people's need for ritual.

Our favorite example of a spontaneous happenstance developed when we were traveling in France in the beginning of a hot, crowded tourist season. We had chosen the quiet "heart of France," the route of Jacques Coeur, just south of Bourges. Away from the hustle and bustle and giant chateaux of the Loire, we focused on the lesser-known castles of Meillant and Ainay-le-Vieil, Georges Sand's hamlet of Nohant, and walks in nearby Colbert's forest.

The day of our anniversary we'd planned a special trip to a flower garden and park with a charming restaurant in a tiny medieval village on the banks of a river, Apremont-sur-Allier, 16 kilometres from Nevers. When we arrived we found the garden and restaurant "Closed on Tuesdays," information which was neglected on the advertising flyer. Slowly we began to revise our day. The riverbank was so quiet and peaceful that we decided to drive to Nevers to gather up a picnic and return. (Perry had actually taken a liking to picnics that year since he'd bought a basket, tiny table and chairs, and a dishcloth as a tablecloth!) We thoroughly enjoyed shopping in the charcuterie, boulangerie, cheese truck, and open-air vegetable and fruit markets. After returning to Apremont we strolled along a fisherman's trail among ferns, shade trees, birds, crickets, and nettles. We toasted one another during our picnic, then painted and slept, listening to sounds of children from school.

About 3:00 we decided to mosey down the road 18 kilometers to St. Augustin, as we'd picked up another flyer advertising an 18th-century chateau in the Bourbonnais style, situated in a nature park, "Open Tuesday-Sunday." As we entered the grounds we were greeted by strange carousel-style band music coming from the interior of the chateau. In the doorway to the salon stood a live eagle; our adventures had only just begun and we let whatever was to happen, happen.

Schoolchildren were clustered all around the grand living room where a multitude of stuffed wild animals stood by or sat in the formal chairs. A school mistress yanked a small boy out of an antique chair, almost smashing into the eagle as she catapulted him out the door, while the music played on. Outside we could choose between long, medium, or short walks—the first circular trails we'd found in France. We could wander under the trees, across meadows, by ponds, among wild and tame animals and birds (both caged and free). This was actually a zoo, similar to those originated by royal families who liked collecting animals on their grand estates. As we strolled along we kept coming upon wonderful sights. First of all, the owner, a battle-axe of a woman wearing African camouflage garb, shuffled along in bedroom slippers, screaming out to her workers to get busy. Deer, ducks, and swans joined one another in a river. Baby sangliers (wild boar) were squealing and shrieking behind a giant wired pen—at older ladies who, with shaking hands, were offering peanuts and getting nipped. A few paces off a camel was losing his coat as he sidled up to a young dromedary; and next to them a male tiger named Lolita lay on his back sleeping peacefully. We walked about three miles like this, coming across animals in the fern forests and out in the fields.

At the end of our journey we sat on a bench beside an ostrich who made a series of belches, and then started chasing another ostrich in circles around us. The zoo owner continued to tromp around in her slippers and shrieked at a wraithe of a woman who was too reticent about selling cold drinks from within her dark kiosk. Suddenly I looked to Perry's left: the eagle was now sitting right next to Perry, staring right into his eyes. We began to laugh—and kept laughing for a long time, appreciating the theater of the absurd. What a wonderful time we were having.

Did you allow for spontaneity within your plan?

What did you like that happened? What didn't you like?

What insights did you gain?

If you didn't allow for spontaneity, what prevented you?

EVALUATING YOUR PLAN ALONG THE WAY

On their last business-and-pleasure trip, Ben and Kitty were getting along better than ever before. At dinner one night they listed some of the reasons that things were going well:

- Ben had reviewed the convention's agenda and decided which meetings or social functions were "musts" for him and which he wanted both of them to attend.
- They discussed their expectations of one another at these functions, including each one's limitations. For example, no more than two hours at social events and each was expected to be appropriately scintillating company only two out of three times.
- They reviewed which topics were acceptable for each of them to discuss and which were off limits.
- They arranged to catch up with one another periodically at social events to compare notes or exchange a brief pat on the shoulder or hug.
- They made plans to spend time together away from Ben's business associates (walks, tours, restaurants, and rests).
- They developed a system by which Ben could rank which values were most important to him (comparing himself personally and professionally with peers, pride in showing Kitty off, enjoyment of travel, business contact with peers, contact with top management, professional status, recognition for the quality and quantity of his work).
- They toasted one another each day over how well they were doing. They discovered that the more they congratulated one another the less they fought and the better they felt both mentally and physically.

For the pleasure portion of a trip in Switzerland, Perry and I wrote down factors contributing to our pleasure and compared them with another trip:

1. We stayed twelve days in one spot. (Last year we'd spent a maximum of five days in one place.)
2. Distances between places were short—20-30 minute drives. (Last year we drove at least two or three hours a day.)
3. Surrounding towns offered historical sites, a folk museum, shops, and open air cafés.
4. No crowds.
5. Not too difficult to find good food with small enough portions. (Last year we ate too much.)
6. Most inhabitants speak English or French.
7. Comfortable accommodations.
8. Desk clerks provided us with excellent ideas and directions for our rambles.
9. Contracts or agreements between us were working well. (Last year we were at odds with one another over our eating and diet.)
10. Both of us were feeling healthy and had similar levels of energy. (Last year Perry felt better than I; my back wasn't yet healed.)
11. Our moods were similar most of the time, or when one of us was down or depressed, the other remained supportive. (Last year I didn't want to travel and Perry did, so I was depressed some of the time.)
12. We were respecting our differences. (What a long way we've come from putting each other down.)

Comparing this trip to earlier ones contributed to our sense of satisfaction. We could see that our glasses were rather full so we didn't need to pressure ourselves to fill glasses that would never be full enough.

Other partners celebrate their achievements in various ways. Marge and Phil toast one another after stopping themselves from discussing subjects they had agreed were forbidden before leaving home. Nina and Matt even send cards of appreciation or notes of congratulations to one another for getting through a hard time.

What did you do when things were going well?

If you celebrated, how did you do it?

If you didn't acknowledge when things were going well what happened—did your trips continue to go well or did you find yourselves going downhill?

WHAT ADJUSTMENTS DID YOU MAKE?

Along the way, you probably had to make adjustments to your plans. How do you decide whose responsibility it is to carry out a plan if one wants to make a change and the other does not?

Perry had planned a drive from Trémolat in the Dordogne country of France to our next stop in Bannegon, just south of Bourges. We had studied the map and had agreed it was a longer drive than usual but that we could manage: "Just one long drive wouldn't hurt." But when we reached Trémolat I had second thoughts. I felt hot and tired from too much driving during the days preceding. I asked Perry how he felt about leaving a day early and making an intermediate one-night stop. He was quite content to keep our plans as they were, but when I offered to research a spot, check it with him, and make the reservations, he agreed to consider a change.

When we arrived, the hotel was indeed *not* up to Perry's snuff; the only available room had a double bed and an additional bunk. (Since I can't stand Perry's snoring, tossing, and turning, and grabbing the blankets, we always ask for twins.) After several rounds of "I'll take the bunk," answered by "No, I will," Perry accepted the double bed, which I offered him to assuage my guilt about changing his plan.

At dinner I listened to his complaints about the ugliness of the wallpaper, the sound of flushing toilets, and the too-thin walls. (He was careful not to blame me.) One of my inner voices said, "You *should* have done better, we never should have done this, you know Perry always makes better plans than you." Another voice chimed in, "Nobody's perfect, you know." I joined Perry in a few good-natured complaints myself. Somehow I'd always thought that if one of us complained the other could not; suddenly we'd turned it into a game and began to chuckle, and ended up saying, "If we didn't have this bad time would we really appreciate all the good ones we've had?" We applauded one another about how well we'd made the decision: The partner who wants to make a change must do the work involved, check with his or her partner along the way so there will be no, "See, I told you so," and there must be room for complaints.

What adjustments did you make along the way?

What did you discover in making them?

DID YOUR TECHNIQUES WORK WHEN YOU WERE ANGRY?

When I'm furious, instead of exploding out loud as in the past, I promised myself to write in my journal. One day, I scribbled:

> I'm *wild*. I went out of my way to help Perry in a difficult situation at the hotel and feel rejected, worthless, useless. Perry only wants to do everything *his* way so why should I try?
>
> Here's what happened. A horrible conference of insurance men were loud, drunk, obnoxious in the hotel last night. I got bothered this time not for myself but for Perry, who complained bitterly but wouldn't *do* anything. So I shouted, "Silenzio," out the window and called the concierge for help. In the morning I quietly composed a letter of complaint to the insurance company

and later I read it to Perry, hoping he would appreciate it. But he disagreed with my method for handling the problem. He wanted to talk with the manager and blame the hotel for what happened. It pisses me off that Perry *won't* appreciate my offer to help. Why does he have to do everything? I. hate feeling beholden.

Now it's later—in the car again and my nasty mood is fading after a good lunch and some humoring by Perry. He'd waited through my furious writing, somewhat like a patient dog, having learned over the ages that if he interrupts me, I'll blow my stack. Just when my energy was slowing down, he asked me if I'd finished and I sighed with relief, closed this book, and announced that I'd read it at dinner, if he was willing to hear it. He said yes and even mentioned that he'd like me to read because we could probably get a good laugh.

At lunch we briefly discussed what we might have to give up if we were to be good company for one another as we grow older together. It's the first time Perry has been willing to consider giving up his hurry: "I have to travel while I can because . . ." And I never know what the "because" is. Because he'll run himself till he drops dead? This time Perry even talked about slowing down to enjoy being in one place for a longer time on vacation. See what my giving up verbal explosions can start! An unexpected pleasure in the long run.

What techniques that you'd planned worked out well for you on the trip?

Were the results what you expected?

HOW DID YOU COPE WITH MINOR PROBLEMS?

Problems of the minor variety can be frustrating. You can greet them with annoyance, amusement, or see them as a challenge from which to learn.

Ethel and Maurice hadn't realized the importance of clean, modern toilet facilities. They found themselves on a day-long walking and sightseeing excursion in Naples. They came across lavatories consisting of holes in the ground, stand-up varieties with two places marked in concrete for their feet, or unsanitary sit-down toilets with scratchy paper thick enough to write notes on. These conditions bothered them enough so that when they arrived in Rome, instead of continuing to complain, they planned for bathroom breaks in hotel and restaurant facilities before setting forth in the morning.

When Sadie and Ray crossed borders from France to Switzerland one year, they expected to breeze through because they always had before and they didn't give it much thought. Sadie found herself suddenly jiggling coins in her pocketbook and talking nervously as the customs official, *the* authority, approached. "Nothing to declare?" he asked in French, followed by a severe look, and questions she thought she understood to be, "How much money do you have? Do you own this car? Why are you taking it across the border?" They were stopped for a long time, holding up cars behind them while the official conferred with a colleague. Sadie suddenly felt small, "Who am I?" She accused herself, "Did I do something wrong? Do they think we've stolen the car? Are we carrying something contraband?" All the times she'd put her hand into the cookie jar, committed misdemeanors, or crossed the limits entered her thoughts. She found herself praying when the official reviewed Ray's papers of car ownership and their passports, "Please see that our faces *are* the same as our photographs. Well, our hair isn't quite the same, smiles are different. But please *see* the likeness." When the passports were returned, Sadie sighed, "Whew! We made the grade." Crossing borders sometimes makes travelers feel a crisis in their identity.

Grace and Jane carefully planned an excursion that included a long walk and return by boat. Before departing they reviewed the boat schedule, then walked for seven hours, and sat waiting an hour for the boat which didn't come. It started to rain and they reread the schedule a third time, then asked the saleslady in the kiosk near the boat dock if it was coming. She nodded. They hoped she really understood their English. They felt stranded when a fellow traveler pointed out that they must walk back today because they hadn't read in small print in German that a sunny smiling face on a schedule meant that the boat makes a stop *only* on sunny days. This pair learned to ask for help in reading a schedule and chalked that trip up to a percentage of time they'd allowed for mistakes.

Joanne and Bart expected to be able to cash her traveler's checks in any bank, or certainly at American Express offices. Joanne suddenly developed a shaking hand because of taking medication. The bank clerk refused to accept her check because her signature did not match how she had signed her name at home. However much she pleaded it was to no avail. Bart couldn't sign the check since it wasn't written in his name, and Joanne was carrying all the checks for both of them since that was one of the responsibilities Joanne agreed to take before leaving home. They went back to the hotel and after a long explanation the clerk was willing to cash Joanne's check—*this* time. However, at the next locale, the same problem arose. They had to wire home for money and learned that next time both of them needed to carry traveler's checks.

Morris and Kathy dreamed for years about how much they would enjoy English pubs. Upon arriving in England they were thrilled to find the outside of the pub buildings, painstakingly painted with inviting signs edged in gold and intriguing names such as *The Nag's Head, The King's Arms, The Nosebag*. However, the interiors were most often dingy and smoky, and the food itself was less than appetizing (soggy meat pies and thick slices of overcooked beef with gravy of wallpaper paste consistency.) They learned that dreams can have a disappointing reality.

One day Perry and I found ourselves in the rain in Florence, Italy, not knowing how to phone for a taxi because we had no tokens and didn't know where to purchase them. Perry thought of a clever solution; we stepped into a leather goods shop to buy a wallet so we could ask the shopkeeper who spoke English to phone for us.

Kirk was very proud of having lost 30 pounds, and to ensure his continuing to maintain his appropriate weight, he had made an agreement with Leila that she would not bribe him with food and would not make disparaging remarks about what he ordered. However, Leila really enjoyed lingering over well-prepared lunches and dinner. Both of them wanted to be sociable and celebrate together during meal times. As Leila relished each bite, Kirk had real difficulty controlling his diet. In his head he heard the voice: "Just this little bit won't matter" just once too often; he succumbed to the sweet, and was angry with his loss of control and Leila's interminable eating process. Through monumental effort each day, Kirk managed to resist many temptations. Leila gave up a few lunches to join him but was unhappy. Kirk learned that he was more patient than he'd ever dreamed possible and knew he needed to ask for help to change his agreement with Leila once they returned home.

Perry and I found ourselves suddenly confronted by a machine with printed instructions for buying train tickets in Switzerland. Perry only had paper money and my coins were stuck somewhere in my knapsack. When I pulled them out, as the train approached,

I could find only small coins (less than a penny each.) We were frantic because the instructions in three languages stated that we would have to pay a heavy fine for riding the train without purchasing a ticket before boarding. The train arrived and we were caught between waiting an hour and a half for the next train while I took my time to figure out which coins to use or hopping aboard with a feeling of guilt, praying the authorities wouldn't catch us. We did jump on. I dreamed up stories of what I'd say if we were discovered. Upon arrival at our destination I placed the correct coins in the machine at that station because we didn't want to accept a free ride. We learned to travel with readily accessible coins, in large enough denominations to put into a machine and decided it would be worthwhile to take time before starting out each day to separate our smaller from larger coins. When we returned home we discovered that one traveler, struck by so many unexpected difficulties and types of problems in Europe, wrote *Travel Key Europe*[3] to deal with such frustrating experiences as coping with coins, tokens, and dial tones for foreign telephones, and details on public transit in European countries.

How did you cope with new problems of the minor variety along the way?

What did you learn about yourself or your partner in handling these problems?

HOW DID YOU COPE WITH THE UNEXPECTED?

Linda and Murphy had been close friends for ten years, had carefully planned their first trip together to the Orient. For part of their stay—a week in Japan—Linda wanted to see as much as possible, visiting one city with three long train trips into the countryside. Murphy wanted to stay in the city and take two short day trips to the country. They compromised and agreed to spend four nights in the city and three in one spot in the country.

When they were actually on their trip they began to fight. Linda wanted Murphy to be more spontaneous and take less time making decisions. Murphy resented Linda's pushing him into a whirlwind

3. Peter Manston, *Travel Key to Europe* (Travel Keys, Box 160691, Sacramento, CA 95816, 1985).

of activity, and he now wanted more time for himself alone. Murphy was the first to break the stalemate by suggesting they each write two complaints about the other as well as two credits about the other's positive attributes or contributions. This helped, although Linda soon grew tired of analyzing the problem in such depth. But Murphy stuck by his decision to spend more time alone, and Linda began to discover places she could visit on her own. They agreed to continue traveling together as long as each agreed to not force the other to conform to "his" or "her" way.

Other partnerships do not fare so well and sometimes the most important point to learn is what values are most dear to you. This may mean that you won't travel with the same partner(s) again. For example, Dan and Karen traveled with Jamie and Lo. Although they thought they had planned carefully, when they were on the trip different values and travel styles emerged. Karen and Dan enjoyed stopping to see beautiful scenery while Jamie and Lo pressed on in a hurry to get to a lake "because it's supposed to be beautiful." Dan and Karen wanted to examine each moment and move at a slow pace, whereas Jamie and Lo made long lists to see and do as much as possible "because that's how we know we're really having a good time." One day Jamie and Lo marched along in a town a block ahead of Karen and Dan, who kept stopping to look and listen. Dan and Karen decided to suggest friendly ways for the couples to separate: "Since we want to poke around slowly and don't want to hold you up, let's make our own plans in the morning and meet for dinner. Or we could go off by ourselves one day and be together the next." The time the foursome spent together remained tense because Jamie and Lo simply wouldn't understand why Dan and Karen didn't want to be with them all the time. But Dan and Karen survived the trip and learned that a weekend twice a year with Jamie and Lo was tolerable but more than that was near disaster.

In another case, Alice discovered that while traveling with her good friend Janet had always been delightful before, when she joined in a trip with Janet's twelve-year-old son everything changed. Janet was unwilling to make any compromises when her child was around, and Alice felt she herself was being treated as a large obstreperous child who was interfering with Janet's plans. When Alice's various attempts at compromise were rebuffed, she focused on what, if anything, could be salvaged from this experience: You can't take *anything* for granted—you can't make assumptions that just because you've gotten along with a friend in one circumstance that you will in another, especially with an additional person along.

How did you cope with change—when reality was very different from what you had expected or planned?

Were you pleased or displeased with your response to the change?

What would you change for "next time"?

HOW DID YOU COPE WITH DIFFERING MOODS?

How did you cope with times when one of you was depressed, for example, and your partner delighted? Peter and Mona had gotten along well for years in their travels. Both professional people, they worked hard during the year and were usually delighted to be away together. But this year, Mona had just retired and she wanted to rest and deal with her uneasiness about what she wanted and could afford to do—to develop a new career or stay retired. She'd agreed to go on the trip because out of the blue, with no just cause, she was afraid that if she didn't go Peter would find another woman. "Well," she humphed, "he'll never find another one who'll give what *I* give." The voice of fear was stilled—for a while.

She felt depressed while Peter was most enthusiastic about their travels and found herself complaining or kicking the dirt. At times she felt badly about not being able to hide her feelings. She was somehow fighting the good time that Peter was trying to provide for them both while she was making a major change in her life. She often felt she didn't deserve to have any more than she had already, but still continued to try hard not to put a damper on Peter's spirit with her sour company. Sometimes, she figured, the best is just to get through the hard times, realize they won't last forever, and say, "I'm doing the best I can in this situation and it isn't easy."

Peter sensed Mona's mood and decided to talk about what was going on from his point of view: "I feel badly about dragging you away. I know you didn't want to come this time and it's hard for you. But I need to get away on this trip." He didn't blame Mona for not wanting the same things he did, and he expressed his pleasure in her being with him. Mona asked him to write notes about what he appreciated about her as a way of warding off the voices of depression,and during the remainder of the trip this technique was highly successful.

Upon returning home Mona proposed that since Peter wanted to travel more often than she did, she really wanted him to look at his options for traveling without her and give her a choice that wouldn't arouse her fearfulness; for instance, "I want to go to Mexico. I'd love for you to come with me but if you don't want to I'll understand. I'll go by myself, or with a friend, or on a tour. And we can review my plans together, so you won't need to worry."

Sometimes you can both start out in the same mood (delighted), but as the trip continues one of you becomes tight and restrained. If the good-humored partner is willing to try breaking the ice by exploring the reasons for the sudden change in mood—rather than starting a fight—and if the partner is willing to talk, you may each make fascinating discoveries.

Martha and Dave were traveling by car toward Yosemite on Highway 49. Martha, who had been smiling over her purchase of a hat adorned with moose antlers in the last shop in a small town, was suddenly aware that Dave was no longer relaxed, nor did he appear in good humor; all was not well. She asked what was the matter. At first Dave simply shook his head, but Martha reassured him that she wouldn't jump on him—she really wanted to know what was going on. Dave explained how he'd carefully plotted out a schedule in his mind before leaving home, listing specifically what they'd have to do in order to reach their destination by 6:00 p.m. He became uncomfortable in the store because the length of time spent there meant they wouldn't get to stop in the next town. But he didn't say anything, since Martha was enjoying her leisure.

Dave had assumed his schedule was obvious and had gotten into a funk when he wasn't getting what he wanted. After Martha explained that he hadn't clearly stated his desires, they began a most interesting comparison of how they each looked at time. On vacation Dave tended to act as he did at work, listing his jobs and how long each would take, whereas Martha was lax about the time in between departure and arrival points. From the discussion, she credited Dave for his skill in time management, and Dave learned that he needed to tell her what he'd planned and not be disappointed if Martha could not read his mind. Because they focused on learning from the experience rather than putting one another down, Dave's humor was restored and they continued their good time together.

What did you do when your partner's moods did not coincide with yours?

Can you spot why your moods differed? Was one of you concerned with a big change in profession or family, something you said or did to annoy your partner, something you didn't ask for and assumed, a difference of values or pacing?

Even if you didn't know the reason, were you able to help one another?

HOW DID YOU COPE WITH UNPLEASANTNESS?

It's difficult when you have carefully planned a trip and the weather refuses to cooperate. You may find yourselves inadequately prepared and without ready alternatives.

Weather

For years Betty and Judd had planned their trip to the Great Barrier Reef. When they were finally able to afford it, they were too late to get reservations on the island of their first choice but settled with pleasure on their second choice, Heron Island. The morning of their departure from the Australian mainland, a lashing storm brought rain and high winds. All the helicopters were grounded, but a seaplane would take them to a boat offshore of the island. At this point they faced a difficult decision: take a chance in this storm and go ahead or stay in the very dull town on the mainland until the storm blew over. Since they'd waited so long to come to the Great Barrier Reef, they decided to take the chance.

With trepidation, they climbed aboard the seaplane with a couple from England who laughed nervously with them upon takeoff. The rough flight worsened when the pilot discovered they were ten miles off course, then corrected his position, and landed in very rough waters near a boat filled with very green-looking members of a TV crew who were about to exchange places with the four sea plane passengers. Betty grabbed Judd's arm, barely letting out a squeal when her luggage swished through the water during the transfer to the boat. The ride to shore was a seasickening adventure and they debarked in the continuing sultry heat, rain, and wind. As they straggled toward the hotel, Betty tripped in giant holes made by birds, one of which took a dive, and barely missed her head. She shrieked, "Goddamn birds! Judd, I *hate* birds." In all their research and planning somehow they had both glossed over information that birds would naturally inhabit Heron Island. Finally in their room, bedraggled, Judd began the clean-up by washing the salt off his shoes, while Betty slammed down the windows in an effort to keep out the swooping birds. She burst into tears, and as Judd tried to comfort her, he noted water flowing into the bedroom—he'd left the tap on in the bathroom. "What to do?" they moaned together, "this is *awful*." They were damned if they'd fly back in this kind of storm, even if they could. At dinner they joined the English couple with whom they commiserated with humor.

The rain continued the following day. To make matters worse, Betty and Judd came across birds regurgitating food and then putting it into the mouths of their mates as well as their young. "This is *the* last straw," screamed Betty, determined to look now at the ground in front of her, one step at a time, avoiding bird holes—back to the hotel to read and write, and then to chat and laugh with the English couple, comparing fears, adventures, and miseries. The next day, under cloudy skies, but no rain, they left the island and later discussed what they'd learned: to inquire about the natural wildlife in an area they planned to visit; not to fly in bad weather; and that under adverse conditions they can bank on their humor and ability to make friends.

Although it can be miserable if you've planned for a vacation in the sun and it rains every day you're away, if you can't afford to move to another locale sometimes there's nothing to do but make the best of it. Perry and I have spent ten days in Hawaii where it rained every day. While many other partners exchanged grim glances and became nastier as the days wore on, we learned how resourceful we were—reading, writing, and painting; walking in the rain in plastic gear; making dolls of sticks, seaweed, and shells; and feeling very competent about what we concocted to have a good time.

If you're close to home you can more easily call it quits during a camping trip when the rain disintegrates your paper hats, or mud surrounds your tent and you're wet and cold. At that time you'll have to decide if you want to be a good sport and rough it or return to the comforts of home.

Sometimes the most important thing to learn is not to put yourself in that situation again. Perry and I become so miserable in the heat that we have learned to avoid traveling to hot spots during summer months. And if we find ourselves in an unexpected hot spell we cut down on our activities and head for water wherever we can find it—if need be, the shower in our hotel. Some partners learn that nothing is worth their discomfort in the heat, especially in cities, and cut their trip short even though far from home.

In early June, Mary and Bill had traveled through high temperatures by car from Positano, in southern Italy, to Rome. They had carefully planned their day around a trip to the Capitoline Museum to view a famed Russian collection of modern paintings. When they checked into their hotel at 4:00 p.m. they were told that the museum reopened at 5:00 p.m. They then proceeded to argue. Bill wanted to wait in line to get a good place, while Mary thought they should first go to the airline office to reconfirm their reservations and make sure they had made a good choice of seating assignments; neither wanted to be left alone. They decided to do it Mary's way. Hot and hassled but determined to reach their goal, they reached the museum a little before 6:00. A line five blocks long had formed.

Mary: No, it's not worth it.

Bill: Oh, yes, we drove all this way and I want to see it.

Mary: (to herself) I'll feel guilty if I leave now, after he came to the airlines with me and it's my fault we're late.

(For five minutes she stands on one foot, then the other, the sun still beating down.)

Bill: Well, o.k. let's leave.

Mary: No, we've waited a while now, we might as well stick it out now. (to herself: "You know, I hate this. I hate cities. I hate this heat. But if I don't see this show people will really think I blew it. You know, with all these crowds you can't see the show anyway.")

Bill: (to himself) I should have listened to her in the first place. I *do* hate museums, goddamn it, but I'll feel too much like a loser if I quit now though, and I hate losing.

(They both stand together, glaring, sighing occasionally. After 15 minutes, with looks of despair:)

Mary: I can't stand it another minute. Maybe we're poor sports but I'm not going to change that. No. (to herself: "It would be better if we traveled with other people some of the time—would take some of this kind of pressure off.")

Bill: Let's go.

(They slump off into the heat and find a taxi.)

Although Mary and Bill did not look at their alternatives in choosing another site—they were hooked on "having to see this because that's what we set out to do"—perhaps it was more important for them to learn that they didn't have to change their compul-

sions, habits, or preferences for countryside, no matter what anyone else thought. It was really all right to plan future itineraries without any cities. They didn't have to suffer heat, metropolises, or museums any longer. And they both agreed in the future, to travel with other people some of the time because that helped them enjoy one another more.

What did you learn about yourselves and one another in unpleasant weather conditions?

Could you use what you learned in other situations?

Losses and Robberies

Trying to prevent robberies is difficult enough but actually suffering a loss can be a crisis. Nola, Alicia, and Bruce traveled in a constant state of what they called "purse panic" because of their own and others' tales of thievery. Each day they went through a ritual ceremony of: (1) putting passport, checks, credit cards, and money into the hotel or pension safe; (2) taking out only what they would need for the day and placing it carefully into purses that hung from their necks (Bruce kept one credit card, checks, and daily money supply in his pants' pocket, which he held together with safety pins); and (3) adding a small change purse containing the equivalent of five dollars to a larger handbag with their journal and maps, in case they needed to give something quickly to a robber. Even so, they each seemed always distracted, clutching a bag, pocket, or neck purse, wondering if all was still intact.

On their last night in Barcelona, Myra and Glen were in romantic moods, having consumed a delicious paella and a bottle of fine wine. As they were walking down a lonely street in the old Gothic quarter admiring the architecture, Myra was suddenly bowled over, and as she fell to her knees her purse was snatched. Glen, outraged and more foolish than brave, ran three blocks after the shadows of two young boys. A third was hidden behind a car, and as Glen was screaming expletives, he was tripped—fortunately—for he might otherwise have disappeared into a dark alley and been mugged himself.

Myra called out a yelping "Help," while Glen came suddenly to his senses: how futile the chase. He returned to Myra and suggested they go back to the hotel, but Myra persuaded him to go to the police station. Later they recalled how like tourists they had appeared—Myra swinging her bag, and both gazing up, carefree—like pigeons, or sitting ducks. They'd not again walk alone, no matter how romantic and colorful the stroll.

The decision to go to the police proved intelligent because, as they later learned, in order to replace a passport or traveler's checks, whether lost or stolen, travelers must *first* file a police report. The next day they heard tale after tale of tourists who had stood waiting in line for a day at American Express only to find they had to go to the police before anything else.

In Italy they learned to never carry their wallets in back pockets, to carry their important cards and money in belts or inside purses, and to leave passports in the hotel safe because of a rash of new tricks developed by gypsies. One involved a gypsy mother whose little girls bumped against an elderly man and pulled up their skirts. While their mother screamed and accused the man of molesting her children, in the confusion, they stole his wallet. When he realized he'd been robbed he took after the mother who had by then grabbed her children to "protect" them from harm. Since she continued screaming as if her darlings had been sexually attacked, the man had to retreat in embarrassment, unable to communicate in Italian. A second game consisted of two gypsies approaching partners with a blank piece of cardboard held above their waists. While the unsuspecting twosome looked curiously at the cardboard, the gypsies' hands were in their pockets and purses. Only those tourists who walked with purpose and determination were able to avoid this trap.

Street beggars may be sincere or hustlers. In Rome Perry and I saw a gypsy mother with her good-looking little son begging for coins from tourists in cafés. We continued walking toward Trastevere for lunch. There, four miles from the cafés, we saw the gypsy boy and his mother enjoying a sumptuous meal at the best restaurant on the piazza.

How did you protect yourselves from loss or robbery?

If you were robbed or lost your passport or checks how did you handle the situation?

What did you learn to pass on as tips to others?

Getting Lost

Losing your way almost always produces anxiety. Even if you've arranged and agreed upon an allowance for mistakes, it's hard to distinguish between "losing yourself" (your identity) and "losing your way." Partners may find themselves asking each other: "Why the hell did we take *that* road? Goddamn it, give me the map."

When Hattie and Pearl entered a station of the London underground, Hattie asked if they now wanted to go north or south. "North," replied Pearl with assurance, having just consulted the map. She marched ahead to the tracks, only to realize that Hattie wasn't following her. "Hattie-e-e-e-e-e," she shrieked, and began to panic. Within two minutes her partner reappeared.

Pearl: *Where* have you been? (accusing)

Hattie: I was just checking the map.

Pearl: But you didn't tell me where you were going.

One of the members of a couple standing by snickered, "It sure sounds like two lost Americans to me," which caused Hattie to bristle and look daggers at Pearl, who had turned her back and muttered to herself: "Why didn't she believe me when I said north?" Later, Pearl asked why Hattie had been so upset. "I hate being found out—not knowing the ropes," she answered. "But is it fair to yourself to expect yourself to know the ropes when you're in a foreign country?" asked Pearl. "No," replied Hattie, beginning to smile, "but I still don't like it."

Perry and I thought it was impossible to get lost in Switzerland because the trails are so well marked—but we managed to lose our way twice. The first time, we came to a fork in the trail, one sign pointed to the right: "Piétons": "For walkers," I said. Another sign to the left read "Schmalz," with a picture of a curve of blue on white background. "Cross-country ski trail, I'm sure," said Perry and we agreed to take it. After we had walked several miles the road came to a dead end. How fortunate we were to find telephone poles that led us to the bottom of the mountain. Much to our surprise we also found a truck with an advertising sign affixed, "Schmalz"—which proved to be the name of a road construction company—a far cry from a cross-country ski trail and worth a good laugh.

The second time we lost our way, in the mountains above Churwalden on the Lenzerheide Pass near Zürich, our adventure proved rich, with a scary beginning. We had taken a chair lift to the top of a peak and had walked down to midmountain for a late lunch in the tiny town of Sartons. As we began what we thought was a continued descent, the trail seemed to climb again. This unexpected ascent was not indicated on the cartoon map we'd studied. (It had been our mistake to have not consulted a detailed map.) I paled at the thought of a more difficult walk than we'd planned, my back was beginning to ache, and we still had far to travel before nightfall. Perry wanted to continue along the marked trail but followed my instinct to backtrack along a less clear-cut path that headed downhill. We soon were at a dead end in the middle of a forest. I held back tears and fright. As Perry started climbing back uphill to meet what he hoped was the main trail, I decided to holler out,

"Hallo-o-o-o-o-o," making my breath last a long time. Perry told me to stop screaming, for who could possibly hear me? but I continued to call out, "He-e-e-e-elp," insisting that there might be someone there, even though I didn't really believe it. Miraculously, on the third call, I heard a return of "Oo-o-o-o-o-o-o-o-o" repeated, and this time Perry joined in with a "Who-o-o-o-o-o-o." As the "Oo-o-o-o-o-o" grew louder, we stumbled and almost tumbled toward it.

The owner of the sound turned out to be a heavy-set peasant gentleman in his seventies, who was sitting on a ledge, wearing what looked like bedroom slippers, and holding a fine walking stick. Having taken one look at me he asked, "Angst?" and I vigorously nodded, recognizing he must mean "anxious." I was. In an effort to demonstrate we were lost I turned my arms and hands toward the sky and shrugged my shoulders. He nodded a reassuring smile and motioned us to follow him through the underbrush. With his stick he pointed up to his tree house, which held his hunting gear. Along the way he spoke in a tongue I had never heard before, but when he announced "Voa Romanche," I recognized the name of the Romansh language. We continued our journey, he in his native parlance and we in ours, in cheerful mutual incomprehension. Down, down, down we went. At a clearing he stopped and pointed to the bottom of the mountain—a trail at last. We shook hands warmly, and off we went, waving goodbye. An hour later, just at sunset, we reached our car.

What did we learn?—(1) Not to depend on luck always being on our side—paying the price of fear and possible harm for a good story is too expensive; (2) not to trust a cartoon map; (3) to stay on marked trails; (4) to develop a margin of error large enough to accommodate *all* our mistakes.

What did you do to prevent yourselves from getting lost?

What did you and your partner do if you got lost?

What knowledge or skills did you acquire as a result?

Language Problems

Foreign language situations usually remain a challenge to be greeted by a mixture of discomfort, fear, shyness, frustration, pride in learning a new skill in communication, or humor if you enjoy playing with language.

Some people begin to study a language before leaving home. Phrase books are popular, but relying on them is not always practical. Jill had buried her nose in a phrase book when she was trying to buy a sweater in a small town in Austria. But she found that composing a sentence like "I would like to buy a blue women's sweater, size 12," took such an interminable length of time that she lost the fun of her purchase. She slammed the book shut and thereafter preferred to observe, point, draw pictures of what she wanted, or improvise in sign language.

Our son, Mark, prefers to try getting along by using English with a French, German, Italian, Spanish, or Japanese accent, sprinkled with a few words and phrases of the foreign language. Although this technique does not always get him what he wants, it provides many hours of laughter over misunderstandings. One weekend, after a business trip, Perry and Mark had misgauged the distance between Paris and St. Malo, had driven far longer than they had planned, ate too much of the gastronomic menu, and had both become terribly sick. Mark gesticulated to the innkeeper that he was cold, trying to get the point across that he needed a blanket for his father. Whatever was the matter with the word "blankette"? The innkeeper simply signaled back as if he, too, were cold, yes, indeed, it was a cold day for traveling.

When Mark asked for some sherry—which he thought he pronounced with utmost care, "My fahzair (father), he would like some *sherry*," (the last word with an accentuated and rolled "r")—he was given Cherry Herring, which Perry detests. Almost completely defeated, Mark gave his last college try and came out a winner. Pointing to his father's shirts, he enunciated "laundry" very clearly with accent. The innkeeper took the clothes and returned them clean the next morning.

Back in Paris, Mark's dysentery worsened, so Perry called the house doctor. At the rap on the door, Mark stumbled across the floor to let him in, dreading yet another round in the battle of French-English. He tried desperately to speak his English with the best of French accents, even with a few French words intertwined; however, the doctor assured him he could speak English, gave him some medicine, and Mark and Perry lived to tell the tale.

Sometimes it takes a long time to figure out what's gone wrong with your use of foreign language. On a trip to the Italian and Austrian Tyrol, every time either of us ordered chocolate ice cream for Perry, he wound up with hot chocolate. I asked Perry to make his order very simple, to leave out any extra words like, "Ummm," and polite phrases such as, "If you will,"—as in: "I'd like 'eis schokolade,' if you will." Still he received hot chocolate.

On one of the last days of the trip I was sure I'd figured out just how to get him what he wanted. The menu was illustrated with coffee ice cream in a tall glass labeled "eis kaffee" and I'd read a list of ice creams under the heading "eis"; I was ready. When the waiter arrived I sat up very tall and straight and pointed very deliberately to the picture of the coffee over vanilla ice cream and then to the word "schokolade," I enunciated very clearly "eis schokolade" and pointed to Perry. For myself, I ordered "eis hasselnuss" (hazelnut) and pointed to myself. I got what I'd ordered but Perry got yet another hot chocolate. Two years later we posed our problem to an English-speaking desk clerk in a Swiss hotel. He explained that if we'd asked for "schokoladeneis" we would have succeeded. Saying "eis" before "schokolade" was misunderstood as "heiss," meaning "hot." At last the mystery was solved.

Sometimes making up games is an amusing way to learn enough of a language to avoid misunderstandings. Perry wanted to avoid the mix-up of "poisson" (fish) and "personne" (person). This year "poussin" (small chicken) had appeared on the menu to add to the confusion. I made a list of vocabulary with alliteration and devised the following phrases and sentences to further accentuate the confusion:

poisson—fish
pousser—push
poussin—small chicken
personnes—persons
puces—fleas
poison—poison
deux poissons pour deux personnes—two fish for two persons
un poussin pour deux personnes—one baby chicken for two persons
Deux personnes poussent le poussin—Two persons push the baby chicken.
Poussez le poisson, s'il vous plâit—Push the fish, please.
Pousson les poissons et les poussins sous la table—Push the fish and the little chickens under the table.
J'ai poussé des puces sous le poussin, pas sous le poisson—I've pushed some fleas under the baby chicken, not under the fish.
Ne poussez pas le poison aux poissons—Don't push the poison onto the fish.
Ne poussez pas le poison au poussin—Don't push the poison onto the baby chicken.

Poussez le poison aux puces—Push the poison onto the fleas.

As we practiced these sentences in French and English, with Perry translating, we laughed until tears rolled down our cheeks. Besides the entertainment, Perry really did learn to differentiate the sounds.

How did you cope with language problems on your trip?

Do you have a favorite story to tell?

Automobiles

How courageous (or sometimes foolish) travelers are who rent a car in England, get lost driving through a town, and sideswipe a parked car as they make a turn to the right and end up on their accustomed right side of the street rather than the accustomed left in England. Morton and Sally decided to take trains after losing their tempers and $500 on a deductible insurance policy.

When Perry and I drove in German-speaking countries trying to ferret our way through towns, we were hopelessly confused by long, difficult to pronounce streetnames, "Ausstellungstrasse," "Stampfenbachstrasse," and "Drahtschmidlisteg." I learned to direct Perry to: "turn right on the 'A' street, left when you come to 'S', and then another right, straight across the 'D' street." "Great," he congratulated me, "brilliant, in fact."

Martin and Penny learned some difficult lessons about buying a car abroad. When they arrived in Marseilles, they discovered that they hadn't been informed of the car dealer's change of address. An angry taxi driver took them round and round in heat and heavy traffic while they struggled through papers and leaflets to find any address they might have overlooked. When the driver finally located the new address, after conferring with a conclave of other taxi drivers, the manager was out to lunch and no one knew when he would return.

An hour and a half later, Martin and Penny were invited into an office almost totally devoid of supplies and furniture save for three chairs and a cold metal desk without drawers. The manager swept his arm and hand grandly across his chest and outward, announcing, "Please sit down." "Hooray," they thought, "he speaks English." But, alas, that kindly greeting was the full extent of his English vocabulary. This threesome spent the next four hours in a mass of red-tape, including trips to and from the customs office at the port. At last, the car was in their possession, the last paper signed, and they drove off. Before they turned the corner they heard an awful roar, like an elephant under the chassis. Because they couldn't bear another minute with the "Please-sit-down" dealer, they continued down the streets—the perfect picture of anxiety, impatience, and exhaustion. Two days later, after taking a chance and driving to the next town, they were pleased to discover that the problem was simple; the delivery truck had put a crimp in the muffler.

The heat on that trip was almost unbearable and as Penny flipped through the car manual to the page that described fans and air-conditioning systems, she longed for such a model. Martin replied, "Too bad we didn't order that kind." At home, six weeks later, their car arrived at the docks and they took it to be cleaned. "How really wonderful," the car detailer remarked, "to have such a fine air-conditioning system!" Martin was floored. "Where?" he asked. "Very simple, these two levers—one on the right, the other on the left—you just push them up to the level you wish," said the detailer. "Oh, *no*," they moaned, "all through the heat wave . . ." It never occurred to them that air-conditioning was a standard feature of the model they had ordered. After a good laugh, they considered taking enough time to match up the manual with the car—and if ever they'd pick up another French car, it would be outside of France; Zurich, Switzerland, came highly recommended.

If you had an automobile on your trip would you travel again by car?

What are the pros and cons of renting a car abroad?

HOW DID YOU AVOID PERFECTIONISM?

If you used an allowance for making mistakes was it realistic and helpful? Or did you and your partner squabble in search of unrealistic perfection?

Our last trip was going so well that we needed to make sure to maintain our allowance for mistakes. I had become enamored with a quiet Roman shop off a busy piazza, which specialized in liquors, honeys, and natural restoratives made in convents and monasteries throughout Italy. I decided to cart back two bottles of *grappa*, an Italian brandy, and two bottles of an amaretto with a somewhat bitter taste—insisting that I could never buy them in the United States. Perry maintained I was crazy because they'd be so heavy, and he wouldn't carry them. "*I* will," I swore, "this may be crazy but it's within my allowance for mistakes." The bottles were, indeed, a nuisance because they leaked and were extremely heavy to lug around airports. But rather than deprecate myself for being "so stupid as to make this purchase," I chuckled to think of how safe my mistake turned out to be compared to what worse I might have managed; Perry agreed.

In that case I knew I was making what could well turn out to be a mistake. Sometimes you won't know it at the time, but having a margin of error relieves pressure and allows you to make mistakes without self-deprecation. Eloise and Mitch had just checked into their London hotel. Mitch took a walk by himself to cool his anxiety because they and their luggage had parted company at Heathrow airport. As he left the room, his last words were: "Be *careful* of English plumbing," thinking of the many times it had broken on prior trips. Alone, Eloise, as if eight years old (though fifty-three), emptied the envelope of rose-scented salts into the tub, turned on the bathwater, felt the warm bath towels on the pipes, and counted to ten while holding the handle down on the old toilet.

Then she sauntered into the bedroom, smoothed her sweater, ploofed the pillows on the bed, and poked into drawers, examining the free stationery and the hotel's Bible but really hoping to find a chocolate mint. At the moment that she opened the last drawer, she looked toward the bathroom and sure enough—water was pouring out onto the floor, into the bedroom and hallway, and out the door. Horrified, she pulled the plug, and dialed the phone for the housekeeper. Her stomach began a slow churn at the awful thought of having to admit her ill-doings. "Oh *dear*," said the housekeeper, in tones that let Eloise know that anything English needs to be handled with extreme care and respect.

Still feeling eight years old, Eloise grabbed some towels and began busily tending to the floor. She wanted to appear abject and hardworking when the housekeeper arrived. The housekeeper looked in, surveyed the scene, dashed out, and brought back a pile of dirty but dry towels. She joined Eloise on the floor, assuring "There, there, don't worry," in response to profuse apologies. Eloise noted that she herself was working harder than the housekeeper, but she wouldn't let up until the housekeeper left the room. Alone again, she couldn't help giggling to herself, "Housekeeper in high heels—this is *such* a safe place to make mischievous mistakes."

About an hour later Mitch walked in. "The phone—did anyone call me?" he asked in a businesslike voice. "Ump-mp," mumbled Eloise hugging her secret and smiling, still eight years old. "Nothing happen?" asked Mitch. "Um hmm," said Eloise and told her story. Mitch stared down at his shoes, squishing a little, and smiled slightly. Eloise gradually grew to her age, fifty-three, realizing that she'd have to pay for the carpet damage, if necessary. "Better a mistake here than between the two of us," she decided. Two days later the carpet was dry and good as new. How rare—a free error, no charge!

Sometimes a mistake will help you realize that you no longer have to keep making the same pattern of errors. After Ben and Kitty's thrill attending the Queen's Presentation of Colours, they found themselves near the top of the stadium with a crowd below moving ever so slowly. Kitty advised, "Ben, take it easy. You're starting to get pushy." He had started to jingle coins in his pockets and was stretching his neck to see who he could pass in line. "We have plenty of time," assured Kitty. Ben waited more than he could bear (two minutes), and without a word, he almost leapt down empty benches in rows below, avoiding crowds in the exit aisles. He arrived at the departure gate ahead of all those in seats below him, and seven minutes ahead of Kitty. At the bottom he waited, impatiently at first, wondering, "Why won't she break a rule or two for Christ's sake?" And then he felt foolish. "Why did I *do* this?" His mind wandered far back in time. His father had taught him: "Let's beat the crowds. You're a fool if you stand around waiting for others. You've gotta be first—ahead of everybody or you'll end up nobody at all." "Well," thought Ben, "times have changed. I don't need to do *that* any more. Besides I've had to wait for Kitty anyway." As she approached she shook her head, "I don't like what you did." "Don't say any more," Ben protested, "I've been thinking about how ridiculous it was to push ahead with such disrespect. I don't like what I did either. It's important I made this mistake though—to learn I no longer have to follow old habits."

If you used an allowance for mistakes what was your attitude toward yourself or your partner?

Which mistakes were you willing to make and learn from?

Was the price worth paying for your mistakes?

If you were perfectionistic what were the results?

HOW DID YOU PLAN FOR REENTRY?

By arranging for a smoother transition than you might have done on earlier trips, you can take some of the pain out of homecoming.

Customs

Many partners fight with each other or the customs officials when their anxieties get the best of them. Barbara and Edmund argued for 45 minutes on the plane homeward bound:

Barbara: Shall I declare *everything* on this form?

Edmund: Yes, *everything.*

Barbara: Even if my coat's worn?

Edmund: Yes, everything.

Barbara: We might have to pay duty. That's ridiculous. I'm not going to declare this watch I'm wearing. No one will ever know.

Edmund: Everything.

(Barbara starts listing all their purchases, adds them up, notes that they've gone over the duty-free limit, and begins striking items from the list to avoid payment.)

Edmund: (peering over her shoulder) What are you doing? Why'd you cross that off?

Barbara: I don't want to pay duty.

Edmund: I will *not* go through the customs line with you and have the official question you and find you guilty. I'm too embarrassed.

Barbara: He won't find out.

Edmund: Look! I don't want to take a chance. It's not worth it. Remember the time in Honolulu when my clothes were stripped off and I had to hand over the pearls you got from Mr. Tokuyama and we didn't know how to declare them and had to leave them behind? I won't go through that again.

Barbara: All right, but I don't like it. I want to get away with something.

Edmund: It's *not* worth it.

Going through customs seems to bring out old guilty feelings in many people, memories of incidents as minor as having "smuggled" a firecracker across the Mexican border. Each individual and each partnership need to examine their attitudes about contraband goods and customs declarations. There can be legal consequences if you are discovered, and bouts of conscience if you are not.

What are ways you used to ease your way through customs?

If you broke the rules, what were the consequences and were they worth it?

What Did You Think About Before Arriving Home?

If you think about what you won't like about coming home, you may be able to think of ways to circumvent the problems or at least make them easier. What can you do if you hate being inundated by phone calls, piles of mail, bills, complaints by members of your family or their caretakers?

- Tell friends that you'll be home four days later than is really true, to give you time first to begin to catch up on jet lag, bills, gardening, and household problems.
- Ask that any complaints from children or caretakers be written down, and postpone problem-solving until you have regained your strength.
- Ask neighbors to sort the mail (magazines, throw-aways, bills, and personal letters) and buy a three-day supply of groceries, in exchange for your providing the same service when they take a trip.
- Divide up the homecoming jobs. One of you can make phone calls to family, friends, and colleagues, while the other pays bills.
- Agree that each of you be allowed to make the transition at your own pace. One may choose to unpack quickly, go through the mail, and go out to shop, while the other moves more leisurely, setting aside two hours each day for a week to catch up on the mail and such.

As part of the transition, partners can take time to discuss what each liked and didn't like about the trip, whether the trip met your criteria for success, how to apply what you learned on vacation to your home and work situations, and how to minimize self-deprecation if your vacation didn't meet your expectations even after careful planning. Talking with friends and family can also help you to assimilate your experiences, deal with letdowns after a particularly good trip, and envision how to keep a vacation alive throughout the year to come. The objective is not only to share your good and bad times but to learn from your mistakes so you don't have to repeat them unless you so choose.

Keeping a trip alive for a year can be a work of art. Many travelers continue to write in their journals after their homecoming while settling down to daily routines. Perry and I exchange a gift of flowers each week in remembrance of a fine trip, and read to each other from our journals each Sunday evening throughout the year. Such activities "do more than evoke the sights and sounds of a trip; they help us vividly to remember our former selves,"[4] to take credit for our moments in time, and to keep humor and perspective to plan our future.

What plans have you made for homecoming to ease the reentry process?

How can you keep your trip alive throughout the year if it was a good one?

What can you learn from your mistakes?

OF WHAT TO BE WARY #2

Throughout the year you might think of what you've discovered on your last trip to add to your list of what to be wary—to pass on to yourselves and fellow travelers:

1. Be wary of giving up on a technique you've devised at home before you've given it a fair trial. But be equally wary of hanging onto a strategy that proves not to work for you over a period of time.
2. Be wary of sky caps or ticket agents affixing baggage tags that don't match your point of destination. Similarly be wary of boarding agents tearing the wrong portion from airline tickets.
3. Be wary of gallantly offering to take someone else's baggage with you unless you're prepared to lug it around by yourself.
4. Be wary of meekly following the crowd in the airport when there's a delay or change in flights. You can often make more efficient headway by leaving the boarding area and phoning to obtain information on alternative flights.
5. Be wary of the temptation to panic in near-disaster situations. Focus on breathing techniques to keep you as stable as possible.
6. Be wary of jet lag. Take measures to prevent it or ask yourselves if you're willing to pay the price of not feeling as well as you might.

4. Thomas Mallon, "Letters Penned to Our Future Selves," *New York Times*, Travel Section, July 21, 1985, p. 41.

7. Be wary of too rigid planning. Allow leeway to take advantage of opportunities that present themselves.
8. Be wary of letting things slide when your trip is going well. Take measures to discuss factors that contribute to your pleasure, congratulate yourselves, and celebrate.
9. Be wary of thinking that being seasoned travelers with well-made plans will save you from having to make compromises or adjustments along the way.
10. Be wary if you want to make a change in plans and your partner doesn't. Be prepared to discuss the change, make the reservations, and allow for complaints.
11. Be wary of unrealistic expectations that your and your partner's moods will always coincide. Try to allow for differences without demanding that your partner be delighted or depressed just because you are.
12. Be wary of trying to discuss inflammatory issues between you or to solve problems on vacation that can better wait till you get home.
13. Be wary of visiting a locale that you have not researched to your satisfaction.
14. Be wary of the trap of thinking you *have* to do x, y, or z—simply because you'd planned on it.
15. Be wary of losses and robberies. Take precautions to care for your valuables in hotel safes and carry your credit cards, checks, and money in an inside purse. Immediately report losses to the local police.
16. Be wary of forgetting the distinction between losing your way and losing yourself. Try to avoid panic and focus on your alternatives.
17. Be wary of the probability of language errors. Keep up your humor by devising games. When in a strange place, look carefully at your surroundings first, then check a map. When ordering food try to keep sentences down to a minimum—for instance, "Cream caramel, please," rather than, "Did I see a caramel custard over there at the next table?"
18. Be all the more wary of perfectionism. Be gentle with yourselves in making mistakes, if you can. Try to respond with humor or realize you can learn something valuable from your errors.
19. Be wary of your expectations. Sometimes your "dream vacation" will be a disappointing reality.
20. Be wary of foreign telephones and public transit. If you can't read the fine print be sure to ask for help.

21. Be wary of the difficulty of reentry when you come home. Give yourself time to adjust. Think of ways to keep a good trip alive during the year or to apply what you have learned to your home or work situation.

What "To Be Warys" have you learned to pass along to yourselves and your friends?

References

GENERAL INFORMATION ABOUT TRAVEL

Cranfield, Ingrid and Richard Harrington, editors. *The International Traveler's Handbook.* Dial Press, New York, 1982.

This reference (I think the finest of its kind) is two books in one: extremely valuable and current articles by experienced travelers on a variety of subjects and a traveler's encyclopedia (bibliography, directory of services, maps, descriptions of climate, currency, health, weights and measures, and foreign vocabulary). Various authors discuss methods of travel for independent persons who want to know not only what sights to see, but also difficulties to anticipate.

Massow, Rosalind. *Travel Easy: The Practical Guide for People Over 50.* American Association of Retired Persons (AARP), Washington, D.C., 1985.

This compendium of basic travel information includes: "Doing Your Homework," "All About Tours," "Cruises—Leisure Afloat," "Medically Speaking," and "Dentally Speaking." Listed in the appendix are state and national tourist and travel offices, recommended reading, and maps of key tourist sites. The book is generally available in bookstores, or you can order from AARP, Book Dept., 400 So. Edward St., Mt. Prospect, IL 60056, or 1909 K St., NW Washington, D.C. 20049.

Zobel, Louise Purwin. *The Travel Writer's Handbook.* Writer's Digest Books, Cincinnati, 1980.

This fine reference, written primarily for travel writers, offers excellent advice for domestic and international travelers, including tips on appropriate apparel for visiting temples and shrines, water restrictions, use of telephone and telegraph service, and procedures if civil war breaks out.

MAGAZINES AND NEWSPAPERS

American Society of Travel Agents (ASTA), 4400 MacArthur Blvd., NW Washington, D.C. 20007, or 4420 Hotel Circle Court, Suite 230, San Diego, CA 92108.

ASTA is the largest travel trade association in the country; its newsletter offers practical information for the independent traveler, articles on places travel professionals like to visit, and news about travel agency services.

European Travel and Life, Inabnit Communications, Inc., Box 855, Farmingdale, NY 11737.

Though generally too fancy for our taste (I don't care to read about the aristocratic life at home with the Duke and Duchess of Roxburghe) Perry and I have found some good tips on European restaurants and shopping in this new magazine.

Geo: Travel and Discover the World, Geo Publishing Corp., 5900 Wilshire Blvd., Los Angeles, CA 90036.

Geo publishes interesting and enjoyable articles about gastronomy, hotels off the beaten track, and museums.

Gourmet Magazine is for travelers who like to combine good taste in food with beautiful places off the beaten track. Perry and I planned one of our most delightful trips in the Italian Tyrol from an article in *Gourmet*.

In Britain, British Tourist Authority, Thames Tower, Black's Road, London W6, or 515 Madison Ave., New York, NY 10022.

This publication provides travelers with up-to-date information on events and exhibits in Britain as well as interesting trips, railway or car, to less touristed areas.

New York Times Travel Section.

If we were asked to recommend only one source of information, we would choose the Sunday *New York Times*. Well-written reports for both budget-minded and extravagant travelers on all aspects of travel: areas to visit; details about hotels, restaurants, shops, countryside; tips for medical assistance, guides, transportation fares.

Smithsonian Magazine, Smithsonian Associates, 900 Jefferson Drive, Washington, D.C. 20560.

This magazine often provides up-to-date information on travel and comprehensive study programs in this country and abroad to meet a variety of tastes and budgets. Interested travelers can contact National Associates, Capital Gallery 455, Smithsonian Institution, Washington, D.C. 20560 for tour and seminar brochures.

MAGAZINE AND NEWSPAPER ARTICLES

Often the best travel writing is done by people who love to write and also happen to travel. The following articles are among those that have appealed to us:

Crisp, Quentin. "Memoirs of a Timorous Traveler." *New York Times,* January 6, 1985, Travel, p. 39.

Crisp vividly describes the experience of leaving the comforts of home and entering unknown territory.

Levine, Robert with Ellen Wolff. "Social Time: The Heartbeat of Culture." *Psychology Today,* March 1985, p. 28.

The authors explain why you must learn about a society's time in order to understand the culture. The meanings of "early" or "late," for example, vary across national borders, and travelers are well advised to learn a foreign country's definitions.

Mellon, Thomas. "Letters Penned to Our Future Selves." *New York Times,* July 21, 1985, Travel, p. 41.

Mellon writes of the evocative power of his travel diaries, which enable him to revisit the person he once was. For travelers who want to keep a diary of their moods and feelings rather than just their itinerary.

Ozick, Cynthia. "Enchantments at First Encounter." *New York Times Magazine,* Part 2, March 17, 1985.

Ozick's beautiful word pictures depict the pleasures of discovering the familiar far away from home: a battered old stoop, a stone, a red bus. The article encourages me to enjoy my observations as I sit waiting in an airport, sipping an iced tea in a city street, or strolling in the mountains.

BOOKS ABOUT TRAVEL: OUR FAVORITES

This list, not exhaustive by any means, includes novels and short stories that we have particularly liked.

Adams, Alice. *Return Trips.* Knopf, New York, 1985.

A collection of fifteen poignant short stories, many of which are about older people who travel a good deal in the U.S., Mexico, and Europe. I like the stories especially as studies of authentic interactions between people and how they cope with problems in their travels.

Fisher, Mary Frances Kennedy. *As They Were*. Vintage Books, New York, 1983.

I especially enjoyed the stories "Three Swiss Inns" and "Two Kitchens in Provence"—wonderful evocations of Europe's sights, sounds, and smells.

McEwan, Ian. *The Comfort of Strangers*. Washington Square Press, New York, 1981.

This mystery thriller describes how a young couple wandering down the labyrinths of canals and alleys in an old European city become dupes in a nasty game—an excellent example of problems travelers encounter when they unwittingly trust strangers.

Mann, Thomas. *Death in Venice and Seven Other Stories*. Vintage Books, Random House, New York, 1930.

Death in Venice is, of course, an acknowledged modern masterpiece, a compelling tale that vividly depicts Venice during a cholera epidemic. The intriguing story of an older man in love from afar with a young boy is set against the most beautiful description I have read of Venice in the heat of summer.

Morris, Jan. *Destinations*. Oxford University Press/Rolling Stone, New York, 1980.

Though wordy, I find Morris's detailed essays very worthwhile, and she captures the historical, political, and personal essence of Washington, D.C., New York, Los Angeles, Delhi, Panama, and Cairo.

Nicolson, Nigel. *Portrait of a Marriage*. Future Publications, MacDonald and Co., London, 1974.

Nicolson, son of Harold Nicolson and Vita Sackville-West, writes of his parents' unconventional marriage "which in some way worked . . . miraculously."

Rosenthal, A. M. and Arthur Geller, editors. *The Sophisticated Traveler: Beloved Cities: Europe*. Villard Books, New York, 1984.

This is a collection of essays and short stories by excellent writers and correspondents for the *New York Times* "caught in the act of enjoying themselves" in their travels. Tips about restaurants, sights to see, prices, and of what to be wary.

Stevenson, Robert Louis. *Travels With a Donkey in the Cévennes*. Various editions.

This classic is a beautiful story of a person who traveled "not to go anywhere but to go, [to] travel for travel's sake—the great affair is to move." Like-minded travelers, especially those who rough it in the wilds, will appreciate seeing themselves in Stevenson's story.

BOOKS ABOUT TRAVEL: ANOTHER'S FAVORITES

Everyone we have interviewed has his or her own special books about travel. The following are my mother, Nell Sinton's choices, which I have selected because of her artistic taste and wide variety of reading and travel experiences throughout the world.

Ames, Evelyn. *A Glimpse of Eden*. Houghton-Mifflin, Boston, 1967.

Interesting detailed descriptions of the countryside and animals.

Bakkar, Elna. *An Island Called California*. University of California Press, Berkeley, 1971.

Outstanding photographs and maps complement an accomplished naturalist's ecological approach to plants and animals, birds, seashore, rivers, streams, and mountains in California.

Basho. *The Narow Road to the Deep North and Other Travel Sketches*. Penguin Paperbooks, New York, 1968.

Basho's charming descriptions, travel sketches, and Zen poetry present an excellent picture of seventeenth-century Japan.

Brenan, Gerald. *South from Granada*. Farrar, Straus, Cudahy, New York, 1957.

Good introduction to Spain's people, their occupations and lives.

Dinesen, Isak. *Out of Africa*. Random House, New York, 1937, 1985.

This superb writer lived in Africa and wrote about her life there in an appealing and sensitive manner.

Jiménez, Juan Ramon. *Platero and I*. University of Texas Press, Austin, 1957.

Jiménez won a Nobel Prize in 1956 for this poignant book about his travels with his donkey.

Macaulay, Rose. *The Towers of Trebizond*. Farrar, Straus, Cudahy, New York, 1957.

This romantic novel includes fascinating local color in Turkey.

Miller, Henry. *The Colossus of Marroussi.* Colt Press, San Francisco, 1941.

A joyous celebration of the people and land of Greece that demonstrates the living magnificence of an ancient land.

Moscoti, Sabatino. *The Face of the Ancient Orient.* Doubleday Anchor Paperback, New York, 1960.

A very absorbing, scholarly book about Near Eastern civilizations, their medicine, philosophies, myths, history, and art.

Prescott, William. *Conquest of Peru.* Mentor, New York, 1961.

An exciting and adventurous book that inspires the reader to learn more about the incredible Inca civilization.

Sitwell, Sacheverell. *Spain.* B. T. Batsford, London, 1950.

Sitwell artistically describes villages, towns, atmosphere, and life in Spain.

Synge, John. *The Aran Islands and Other Writings.* Vintage Press, New York, 1962.

A personal and artistic account of primitive Irish life in a bleak landscape.

TIPS FOR TRAVELERS

Tips for travelers appear in newspaper articles, pamphlets, magazines, and books. The following are particularly useful:

American Society of Travel Agents. "Packing Tips." ASTA World Headquarters, 4400 MacArthur Blvd., NW Washington, D.C. 20007.

This brochure provides tips on how to choose luggage, plan your wardrobe, pack efficiently, and insure against theft.

Bender, Marilyn. "Two for the Road." *New York Times,* December 4, 1984, Travel, p. 45.

This article profiles the Travel Companion Exchange (P.O. Box 833, Amityville, NY 11701), which matches prospective travel partners through a questionnaire that determines compatibility. Bender casts her vote for a child—someone too old for a babysitter and too young to vote—as the ideal companion for an adventurous trip that might be too difficult for an older person alone.

Braganti, Nancy L. and Elizabeth Devine. *The Traveler's Guide to European Customs and Manners*. Meadowbrook Books, Deephaven, MN, 1984.

A guide to help American travelers stay out of trouble by learning which behaviors might be misinterpreted by Europeans. Includes specific suggestions for coping with foreign-language problems.

Grimes, Paul. *The New York Times Practical Traveler.* Times Books, New York, 1985.

This outstanding compilation of Grimes' articles in the Sunday Travel Section is our favorite book of travel tips, which include: hotels, insurance, travel agents, traveling with kids or pets, tours, special discounts, medical emergencies, car rentals, luggage, charters, tipping, driving abroad, "creative" air travel, and rules for avoiding common mistakes.

Hoffman, Paul. "They've Got a Little List." *New York Times*, January 20, 1985, Travel, p. 41.

Hoffman describes a 4-page, 194-point astoundingly detailed guide, "Vacation Checklist for Unencumbered Holidays," available from the Motzko Bookstore in Salzburg, Austria. Suggestions include timetables for predeparture tasks (e.g., visits to doctors and dentists, passports, bills, car arrangements, hiding a second set of car keys, and extra cash).

Kowet, Don. *The Jet Lag Book.* Crown Publishing Co., New York, 1983.

Humorous and useful ideas and tips based on up-to-date research on avoiding jet lag.

Manston, Peter B. *Travel Key Europe.* Travel Keys, Sacramento, 1985.

This 320-page book, which can be slipped into a pocket or purse, addresses many types of problems: how to use European pay telephones, find details on public transportation in fourteen major cities, locate and use public toilets, avoid highway speed traps, and cope with foreign language. (Can be ordered from the publisher, Box 160691, Sacramento, CA 95816).

MEDICAL ASSISTANCE

Dahl, Jonathan. "What Happens When a Traveler Needs a Doctor." *Wall Street Journal*, August 1, 1985.

Dahl discusses the advantages and drawbacks, restrictions, and costs of medical assistance programs for travelers abroad. Some programs listed are:

Healthcare Abroad, 923 Investment Building, 1511 K St., NW Washington, D.C. 20005

Europe Assistance Worldwide Services Inc., 2100 Pennsylvania Ave., Suite 617, Washington, D.C. 20037

International Association for Medical Assistance to Travelers, 736 Center St., Lewiston, NY 14092.

This association offers a free directory of doctors and medical centers in 125 countries and territories. Doctors who belong to this association agree to a set payment schedule for memebers ($20 for office visits, $25 for house or hotel visits). Travelers are advised to write for information six to eight weeks before leaving for overseas.

TRAVEL NEWSLETTERS

Alcorn, Sam. "Travel Letters Spot the Offbeat and Exclusive: Your Money Matters." *Wall Street Journal*, July 25, 1985.

A guide to newsletters that supply specialized information about a particular area or activity. (Newletters tend to have more current firsthand information on airfares, restaurants, and political climate than guidebooks and most travel agents.) The *Oxbridge Directory of Newsletters*, found in most libraries, lists 73 travel newsletters, although those published by state or local agencies are not always objective. Alcorn recommends:

La Belle France—focuses on France, most especially current restaurants.

Linksletter—directs travelers to the best golf courses around the world.

Entrée—restaurants and small hotels as yet undiscovered by tourists.

Family Travel Times—vacation spots where children are welcome.

Hideaway Report—tallies complaints and praises of airline passengers, independently selects spots to be reviewed.

Ocean and Cruise News—critiques ship's layout and food along with recommendations.

Travel Smart—offers information for the budget-conscious traveler who wants quality at bargain prices; cautions those on religious tours to watch for low-grade accommodations.

General Newsletters

The following newsletters are among those Perry has researched:

Colen, Bruce David, editor. "The Good Life—A Dining and Travel Newsletter." 27400 Pacific Coast Highway, Malibu, CA 90265.

This newsletter offers Europe-bound travelers advice and recommendations for restaurants, airlines, duty-free shops, wines, hotels, and bookstores. Will probably appeal to the Los Angeles "Jet Set" more than any other group.

Collard, Peter, editor. "The Villa Report." P.O. Box 4101, Greenwich, CT 06830.

This report lists private vacation villas in France and Italy for travelers who can afford luxurious trips and require the services of a maid, cook, and chauffeur.

Harper, Andrew. "Hideaway Report." Harper Associates, Drawer 300, Fairfax Station, VA 22039.

A well-researched and updated guide to peaceful and unspoiled places around the world.

Keown, Ian. "Very Special Places." Very Special Places, Inc., Box 3885, New York, NY 10185.

Reliable, exceptionally interesting and detailed information on inns, resorts, hotels, and hideaways in the Caribbean and Europe.

"Romantic Dining and Travel Letter." P.O. Box 837, Belvedere, CA 94920.

This travel letter includes descriptions of hideaways, roads, bicycling trips, countryside, dining, and wines in the western U.S., with some coverage of trips to Mexico and Europe.

Specialized Newsletters

Various newsletters provide information solely on one city or region; for example, we have just come across a new one:

"London Traveletter." Siewert Publications Ltd., P.O. Box 662, London W10, England 6EW, or Box 10221, Lubbock, TX 79408.

This well-written newsletter provides up-to-date detailed information about unusual British attractions, London specialties (including hairdressers and shops), escapes into the country, stately homes, hotels and inns, restaurants, and entertainment. This publisher also produces "Work and Travel Abroad" for overseas Americans and international travelers.

Newsletters Published by Travel Agencies and Bookstores

Some travel agencies and bookstores publish their own newsletters.

"Insights." Travel Arts Inc., 47 Kearny St., San Francisco, CA 94108.

Articles on expeditions, travel tips, and recommended books.

"The Eye Speaks." The Eye Hears Bookstore, Sarky Square, 1207 F Bridgeway, Sausalito, CA 94965.

Recommendations for expeditions such as caves in the French Dordogne, Greek island tours, houseboats in Kashmir, and a culinary tour of Canton, China; information about savings on the French railways, Eurail passes, and hotels at reasonable prices in places as diverse as New York City and Ashland, Oregon.

GUIDEBOOKS

We caution you to buy up-to-date guidebooks. Nothing is more frustrating than planning a visit to a museum or castle only to find it closed for the day or no longer in existence.

Binns, Richard. *France à la Carte*, 1982-83; *French Leave 3*, 1983 (updated 1985); *Hidden France*, 1982. Ticknor and Fields, 383 Orange St., New Haven, CT 06511, or Chiltern House Publisher's Ltd., Great Britain.

Our very favorite series of guides to France for the independent traveler who recognizes and benefits from specialties off the beaten track—savory sights, sounds, and tastes of rural France. The author writes beautiful descriptions of parts of France least visited by tourists, and he updates the series every two to three years. Hotels and restaurants are listed by regions, with insightful comments about food; eating out disasters are discussed along with eating out delights.

FFRP French Government Tourist Office, 178 Picadilly, London W1V, England OAL.

Guidebooks here are printed in English.

Grimes, Paul, "Practical Traveler: A Guide to Some 1985 Guidebooks," *New York Times* Travel Section, June, 1985.

Grimes recommends:

Éditions Berlitz. Macmillan Publishing Co., 866 Third Ave., NY 10022—guides, travel kits, menu readers.

Fisher Annotated Travel Guides. 401 Broadway, Suite 2300, NY 10013. These books have a knowledgeable but friendly tone with such advice as: "The best meal on British trains is breakfast," and "Buy a raincoat in London rather than packing one before you leave."

Hildebrand Travel Guides. Hippocrene Books, 171 Madison Ave., NY 10016. Books cover countries where tourism is relatively new but growing rapidly. Often ignored by larger publishers, these guides are filled with photographs, local restaurant specialties, and notes for bird watchers.

Insight Guides. Prentice Hall, Route 9W, Englewood Cliffs, NJ 07632. Illustrated guides to various parts of the world.

World at Its Best. Passport Books, National Textbook Co., 4255 West Touhy Ave., Lincolnwood, IL 60646. A series of country guidebooks by Robert S. Kane.

Guide to National Trust Properties in Britain. Automobile Association/British Tourist Authority, 64 St. James St., London SW1, England, 1985. (Check for recent publications.)

This guide leads travelers to old manor houses and gardens that have been bought and kept up by the government. Includes days and times of opening and closing, and whether reservations are required.

Michelin Series—green guides.

The green "Miche" guides provide detailed information on geography, history, art, architecture, and principal sights, with a rating system for European travelers. These guides are inclusive and painstakingly accurate, but the text is endlessly dull.

Michelin Series—red guides.

The single most useful source for recommendations for hotels, restaurants, and sights in most European countries. Includes town plans and mileage between cities and towns, and lists car agents and telephone numbers. Hotels are rated by comfort, atmosphere, and setting, with detailed lists of facilities and prices. Restaurants are rated by excellence of cuisine, with indications of good food at moderate prices. We have rarely been disappointed by recommendations in this series.

Olmsted, Gerald W. *The Morrow Guide to Backcountry Europe.* Quill, New York, 1982.

A guide for travelers who want to wander through Europe's backcountry studying differences among cultures and people. Advice on how to travel as the local inhabitants do (public transportation and on foot).

Steinbicker, Earl. *Day Trips from London.* Hastings House Publishers, New York, 1985.

Fifty detailed trips to appeal to a wide variety of interests: cathedrals, castles, country walks, maritime museums, canals, caves, Roman ruins, historical sites, fishing villages, and spas. All the destinations can be reached by Britrail trains, by bus, or by car.

Steinbicker, Earl. *Day Trips in Germany.* Hastings House Publishers, New York, 1984.

Steinbicker divides Germany into three broad areas and selects one major city in each (Munich, Frankfurt, and Hamburg) to serve as a base for day trips. For example, you can spend one day walking high in the Alps, the next rambling through a city, and the third visiting a medieval town.

HOTEL AND INN GUIDES

In order to avoid disappointment, you might try to find at least two sources that recommend the same hotel or inn.

Brown, Karen. *English, Welsh, and Scottish Country Inns and Castle Hotels.* Travel Press, San Mateo, CA, 1980.

This travel guide for motorists and ramblers includes ten itineraries and descriptions of over one hundred small, special hotels and country inns. The author works in a travel service, plans and personally supervises special itineraries and menus along the way, and updates her recommendations every two or three years. Brown has also published: *French Country Inns and Château Hotels* (1982); and *Inns of Austria, Germany, and Switzerland* is in the research stage. (To order directly from the publisher, write 16 E. Third Ave, Suite 1A, San Mateo, CA 94401).

Châteaux Hotels Indépendents et Hostelleries d'Atmosphère. Herissey, Evreux, France, 1985. (Available from French Government Tourist Bureau, 178 Picadilly, London W1V, England OAL.)

This brochure is written in French but is easy to comprehend in English because of the magnified maps, photographs, and picture symbols to indicate activities and types of accommodations. Hotels and restaurants are classified according to their standards. Guests can stay in small castles, inns, and manor houses, or mills in historical settings.

Harper, Andrew. *The Harper Collection.* Harper Associates, Inc., Drawer 300, Fairfax Station, VA, 22039, 1985.

This collection of hideaway hotels, resorts, rental villas, and restaurants in various parts of the world is based on the author's newsletter. By subscribing to the collection you receive updated information that can be placed in an expandable binder. The accomodations are situated in beautiful areas. Although Harper's recommendations are for travelers on a generous budget, you can always travel to the same area, stay in less expensive inns or campgrounds, and dine in one of the hideaway restaurants for a special treat.

Relais du Silence [Silent Hotels]. Hotel Les Oiseaux, 38640 Claix, France.

This brochure lists French hotels that are reasonably priced, peaceful, and clean, often in untouristed areas. The text, in French, is easy to understand because of maps, photographs, and picture symbols.

Relais et Châteaux. Available from Hotel de Crillon, 10 Place de la Concorde, 75008 Paris, France, or David Mitchell and Co., 200 Madison Ave., New York, NY 10016.

This guide lists 337 calm, comfortable, and welcoming hotels around the world that live up to their reputation and intention to remain old-fashioned, while "tending the body to please the soul." Prices range from moderate to very expensive and the food is generally of very high quality. The French text is easy to comprehend.

Signpost Colour Hotel Guide. Signpost Ltd., Fountain Court, Steelhouse Lane, Birmingham, England B4 6DT.

This guide, updated yearly, provides colored illustrations, prices, and descriptions for recommended hotels in the British Isles. We use this book when we read about a hotel in a magazine or newspaper and want a "second opinion."

Simpson, Norman T. *Country Inn Backroads.* Berkshire Traveller Press, Stockbridge, MA, 1985.

This book on New England, East Coast, Canada, Middle Atlantic, South, Midwest, and the Rocky Mountains, is rewritten and revised each spring. Inns throughout North America are carefully chosen by the author, who visits with almost every innkeeper each year. Simpson cheerfully sprinkles anecdotes among directions, maps, phone numbers, and recreational and cultural attractions. The Berkshire Traveller Press also publishes books on country inns and back roads in Europe as well as travel and country living in the U.S.

Zellers, Margaret. *Switzerland: The Inn Way.* Geomedia Productions, Southport, CT, 1980.

Zellers prefers Switzerland to other countries because "there is no place I know in the world today where things work as dependably as they do in this country." She has visited all the charming inns she recommends. Our favorites were the Hotel Guarda Val in Sporz and the Hotel Vieux Manoir Au Lac in Murten-Meyriez.

MAPS

The best maps are usually found in local bookstores in the area you're visiting. To obtain maps before you go, the best source we know is:

Travel Centers of the World: Reference Catalogue. Box 1673-M, Hollywood, CA 90078.

This 350-page illustrated book lists travel guides and maps of every kind for use all over the world: cities, roads, streets, country, touring, regional, walking, hiking, physical, political, topographic, and aeronautical.

England

Ordnance Survey Maps. Romsey Road, Maybush, Southampton, England S09 4DH.

Maps with a scale of 1:50,000 (1 1/4" to 1 mile) are good for motoring or walking in town but not detailed enough for walking in the countryside. For country rambles use maps scaled 1:25,000 (2 1/2" to 1 mile). Local bookshops also sell even more detailed maps showing paths, rights of way, camping sites, viewpoints, and mountain rescue posts.

Drinkwater, Peter and Harry Hargreaves. *Rambling in the Cotswolds.* Thornhill Press, Cheltenham, England, 1981.

Contains reproduced ordnance survey maps.

Walker's Britain. Pan Books Ltd., London, England, 1982.

This pocket guide to over 240 walks and rambles was created by a team of writers, each an expert in a particular area. Trips are described for walkers of varying abilities—from two to fifteen miles; also includes detailed maps and information on proper footwear and safety rules. This guide is available from Pan Books Ltd., Cavaye Place, London SW10, England 9PG, and Ordnance Survey, Romsey Road, Maybush, Southampton, England SO9 4DH.

France

Institut Géographique Nationale (IGN). 136 bis, rue de Grenelle, 75700 Paris, or 107 rue la Bóetie, 75008, Paris, France.

Maps with a scale of 1:100,000 (1 1/4" to 2 miles). These maps are good for motoring and walking.

Michelin. "Environs de Paris, Sports et Loisirs de Plein Air," Pneu Michelin, 46 Av. de Breteuil, 75341, Paris, France.

This map is our favorite, a guide to sports and leisure activities in the outskirts of Paris (zoos, horseback paths, golf, camping, canoeing, skating, boating, long and short paths for ramblers).

RAMBLING

Though information on rambling is often best found in local bookstores in the areas you'll be visiting, you can purchase series or single books on various walks or rambles before your trip.

Books

Evans, Craig. *On Foot Through Europe*. Quill Books, New York, 1982.

This series includes: *A Trail Guide to Europe's Long-Distance Footpaths* and individual trail guides to Austria, Switzerland, and Lichtenstein; West Germany; the British Isles; Scandinavia; Spain and Portugal; and France and the Benelux nations. Each volume is a comprehensive reference for the hiker—describing every aspect of walking, backpacking, climbing, and ski touring. Evans provides tips on how to plan your hikes and follow trails safely, what to do in emergencies, what equipment to bring, which guidebooks to buy, and where to stay. The walks vary in length and difficulty, ranging from four to five hours to ten-day treks.

Jones, J. Sydney. *Tramping in Europe*. Prentice Hall, Englewood Cliffs, 1984.

Most of the walks described are tours on long distance paths, but all can be broken up into shorter day trips. Ramblers can enjoy camping or choose the comforts of hotels and inns in European countries.

Landes, Alison and Sonia Landes. *Paris Walks*. Holt, Rinehart and Winston, New York, 1981.
Holler, Anne. *Florence Walks*. 1983.
Jones, J. Sydney. *Vienna Walks*. 1981.
Powell, Anton. *London Walks*. 1981.
Rosovsky, Nitza. *Jerusalem Walks*. 1982.
Shetterly, Anya M. *Rome Walks*. 1984.
The publishers are planning forthcoming books on walks in Amsterdam and Montreal.

Each book offers step-by-step tours of the oldest and most fascinating neighborhoods for travelers who like to ramble. (Tip: On Sundays and holidays the streets are quieter and traffic less hectic.) These books encourage walkers to enter into the spirit of neighborhoods rather than visit only a city's historical monuments.

Oakes, George W. *Turn Right at the Fountain.* Holt, Rinehart and Winston, New York, 1965.

This book, periodically revised, was developed from a series of articles in the *New York Times.* Since Oakes' death, new material is provided by Alexandra Chapman to guide the rambler through twenty-one European cities.

Spring, Ira and Harvey Edwards. *100 Hikes in the Alps.* The Mountaineers, 719 Pike St., Seattle, WA, 98101.

The hikes in this book range from day trips to week-long backpack trips through magnificent mountains. Most walks were too challenging for us, but we enjoyed an afternoon's worth of the easier ones.

Brochures, Booklets, and Other Resources

Climber and Rambler Magazine. Holmes McDougall Ltd., Ravenseft House, 302-304 St. Vincent Street, Glasgow, Scotland, G2 5NL.

This magazine is written for rock climbers and provides information on equipment and exciting climbs in various parts of the world. The climbs, while fascinating, are only for the most gung-ho of hikers. However, the areas surrounding the climbs are beautiful and we have been able to ramble leisurely on trails at the base of rock walls.

De Haan, Vicki. *Hiking Trails of the Boulder Mountain Area.* Pruett Publishing Co., Boulder, 1979.

An example of the many booklets in the U.S. and abroad, found in local bookstores. This guide for ramblers takes you through deep woods and meadows on easy trails from a half to five miles long.

Discovering Walks. Shire Publications, 1985. Available from Cromwell House, Princes Risborough, Aylesbury, Buckinghamshire, England HP17 9AJ.

This series of booklets is ideal for ramblers arriving by car to North London and the countryside of England. Each booklet contains ten circular walks with maps and detailed descriptions of unusual aspects; ramblers may choose to do all, or parts of the trips according to their ability and time available.

Fisher, Michael. *Rutland Rambles*. Speigl Press, 4 St. Mary's Place, Stamford, Lincolnshire, England, 1982.

This booklet is a typical example of guides you can find in local bookshops while rambling—these pictorial walks direct you to shops, restaurants, and special places of interest in small towns, as well as walks in the area around Rutland Waters.

Goddard, Donald. "Footloose in Britain: Group Walks Gain Ground in London." *New York Times*, May 26, 1985, Travel, pp. 14, 27.

This article describes the delights of twenty-six inexpensive walking tours of London led by June Street ($2.50-$3.75 per person, per day).

The Great Outdoors. Ravenseft House, 302-304 St. Vincent Street, Glasgow, Scotland, G2 5NL.

This publication provides detailed, up-to-date information about maps and mapmaking for ordnance survey work, reports on the Ramblers' Association, youth hostels, wild-country camping, biking, and short walks to curious places in the countryside of Britain and occasionally other parts of the world.

Hatts, Leigh and Ron Pigram. *Country Walks*. London Transport, 55 Broadway, London SW1.

Sensible directions lead ramblers to some of the best walking around London, and walks are precisely described.

"Out in the Country." Countryside Commission Publications Dispatch Dept., 19-23 Albert Road, Manchester, England.

This booklet, the only one of its kind, lets ramblers know where they can picnic safely in England and Wales without worry of being kicked off the property.

Spurbooks Footpath Guide. Spurbooks Ltd., 1976. Available from publisher at 6 Parade Court, Bourne End, Buckinghamshire, England.

This excellent series of booklets is updated every two or three years.

Ramblers' Association, 1/5 Wandsworth Road, London SW8, England 2LJ.

The association provides booklets, brochures, and tours for ramblers in England who want to walk independently or with groups. The major purpose of the association is to help walkers enjoy strolls and hikes by preserving their rights-of-way through public paths on private property and by making paths walkable and easy to follow. This is also a lobby group of conservationists who take special interest in long distance footpaths and ordnance survey maps.

Topo-Guide du Sentier de Grande Randonée. Available from McCarta Ltd., 122 Kings Cross Road, London WC1X, England, 9D5 (English), or Comité des Sentiers de G.R., 92 rue de Clignancourt, 75883 Paris, Cedex 18, France.

This series of booklets, updated every two or three years, describes hiking paths through France, with cafés, restaurants, and detailed maps of each region. Text is in French.

Warne Garrard Guides for Walkers. Frederick Warne Publishers, Ltd., 1979. Available from publisher at 40 Bedford Square, London WC1B, England 3HE.

These guides of thirty circular walks contain some local history, geography, and ordnance survey maps that are updated each year and posted outside town halls in villages. Readers are encouraged to inform the publishers if they discover errors, though care has been taken to provide only accurate information. Our favorite in this series is Peter A. Price, *Walks for Motorists: Cotswolds Northern Area.*

Westacott, H.D. and Mark Richards. *The Penguin Footpath Guides.* Penguin Books, New York, 1983.

This carefully researched series contains a guide accompanied by nature notes on the profusion of flowers, plants, and trees along the way, as well as details of architecture and local history. Authors also point out when it's worth exploring off the beaten track to pursue a special interest.

BOOKSTORES

Banana Republic Traveler's Bookstore, 224 Grant Ave., San Francisco, CA 94108.

Along with popular Fodor, Michelin, and Frommer guides, the Banana Republic carries many small press and travel guides, language tapes, color-coded maps of wine and cheese areas of France, bilingual menus, and art books. Materials are primarily for travelers who want to learn about the people and countries they plan to visit.

Book Passage, 57 Post St., Suite 401, San Francisco, CA 94104.

Books range from guides to coffee table editions on Sikkim to esoteria on Iowa—for the armchair traveler and the true explorer.

Bradt Enterprises, Inc., 95 Harvey St., Cambridge MA 02140.

Off-beat guidebooks and maps, particularly on Latin America, are the specialty of this mail-order house.

The Complete Traveller, 199 Madison Ave., New York, NY 10016.

This bookstore will ship material which you can order by phone (212-685-9007).

Easy Going, Shattuck Commons, 1400 Shattuck Ave., Berkeley, CA 94709 (Also 1617 Locust St., Walnut Creek, CA 94596.)

These bookstores offer up-to-date information about trips, luggage, and unusual functional items (calculators for currency exchanges, wind-up razors that require no batteries or electricity, even disposable underwear).

The Eye Hears, Sarky Square 1207 F Bridgeway, Sausalito, CA 94965.

This store has a large collection of fiction and nonfiction books about many areas around the globe. It also has a selection of guidebooks, travel survival kits for lesser known locales, and how to travel on a shoestring in Africa and various parts of Asia. Books are published by well-known companies as well as by lesser known small or privately owned presses.

Forsyth Travel Library, P.O. Box 2975, 9154 West 57th St., Shawnee Mission, KS 66201.

Mail order is this bookstore's principal business.

Lonely Planet Publications, P.O. Box 2001A, Berkeley, CA 94702.

Though not a bookstore, this small publisher sends a catalogue upon request and accepts mail-order payment by credit card for Survival Kit guidebooks on India, South and Southeast Asia, the Far East, Australia, Canada, Mexico, and Turkey.

Sandmeyer's Bookstore, 714 South Dearborn St., Chicago, IL 60605.

This store has a collection of out-of-the-ordinary travel books, available by mail order.

The Travel Bookshop, 13 Blenheim Crescent, London W11, England.

This shop carries old and new travel books about every country in the world. Drawings, old maps, and ads for 1890s hotels and cure-alls can be found in this delightful shop.

Travel Books Unlimited, 4931 Cordell Ave., Bethesda, MD 20814.

Unusual guidebooks for the independent traveler.

Traveller's Bookstore, 75 Rockefeller Plaza, 22 W. 52nd St., New York, NY 10019.

Esquire magazine has acknowledged this bookstore as "the best travel bookstore on this continent." Guides, language books and maps, nonfiction and fiction, coffee-table books, and travel log journals are arranged by geographical area. Guidebooks are described and briefly annotated in the store's "Guide to Guidebooks."

Wayfarer Books, P.O. Box 1121, Davenport, IA 52805.

Catalogues available upon request; accepts mail-order payment by credit card.

World Wide Products, 401 NE 45th St., Seattle, WA 98105.

This bookstore handles mail orders as their principal business.

CREATIVE BEHAVIOR PROCESS FOR SOLVING PROBLEMS

The following sources of references are for readers interested in learning more about the background, theory, and application of the Creative Behavior Process which I've used for problem solving throughout this book:

Biestman, Margot; with Mark Brucker, Lisa Hunter, and Anne Smith. *ICAD 1965-1985: A Guide for Integrating a Creative Behavior Class*. Institute for Creative and Artistic Development, Oakland, CA, 1985.

This booklet describes specific techniques used in classes for adults interested in personal growth and in the helping professions (teachers, therapists, social workers, doctors, nurses), as well as artists and writers. Available from ICAD, 5935 Manchester Dr., Oakland, CA 94618.

Newton, Fred E., Jay Greenwood, and Juanita B. Sagan. *Alternatives to Failure: Resources for Improving Teaching. A Report of Two Alternative Classrooms*. Multnomah County Education Service District, Portland, OR, 1985.

The authors present the theory on which the Creative Behavior Process is based in order to report on an experimental program in two junior high schools. Copies of this report are available by written request to Dr. Newton, Multnomah County Education Service District, 220 SE 102nd Ave., Portland, OR 97216.

Pothier, Patricia C., editor. *Psychiatric Nursing: A Basic Text.* Little Brown, 1980.

In chapter 5.1 (pp. 71–78), Pothier discusses the importance of the awareness of the self as she uses the Creative Behavior Process in the field of nursing. She describes characteristics, steps, and skills used in the process, as well as examples of significant experiences in her own development.

Sagan, Juanita B. *ICAD 1965-1985: Overview: Application of Creative Behavior.* Institute for Creative and Artistic Development, Oakland, CA, 1985.

The director of this institute and her husband describe the background of the Creative Behavior Process. Essays by members of ICAD specify how the process has been used personally and interpersonally with family and friends, as well as in a variety of professional situations. May be ordered from ICAD, 5935 Manchester Drive, Oakland, CA 94618.

Index

ABOUT THE AUTHOR

The author and her husband have traveled extensively throughout this country, Europe, North and Central America, and the Far East. Over the course of their thirty-four years of marriage, they have developed a real team approach to vacation and travel. In this book the author's artistry in teaching interpersonal problem-solving skills to people of many different ages, backgrounds, and experiences is complemented by her husband's knowledge of travel resources and his special skill in planning techniques.

For the past twenty-five years, the author has taught and consulted in nursery and elementary schools in the San Francisco Bay Area, and has trained parents, teachers, supervisors, and administrators in national education projects in seventeen urban and rural school districts throughout the United States. Her students have ranged in age from 3 to 93. She has written six books in the field of education and is currently teaching older adults in Oakland, California.

In this, her first book for the general public, the author uses the Creative Behavior Teaching and Learning Process which is designed to lead children and adults to increase satisfaction in their personal, interpersonal, and professional lives through creative self-discovery, decision-making, and problem-solving.

The author and her husband live in Sausalito, California. They have three grown children, two daughters-in-law, a son-in-law-to-be, and two grandchildren.

Order Form

Pèrgot Press

1001 J Bridgeway, Suite 227

Sausalito, CA 94965

Telephone: (415) 332-0279

Please send me the following book by Margot S. Biestman:

______ copies of *Travel For Two: The Art of Compromise* at $10.95 each. I understand that I may return any book for a full refund if not satisfied.

Name ____

Address ____

City ____

State ______________________________ Zip ______________

Californians: Please add 6% sales tax: **$10.95**
.66
$11.61

Shipping: $1.00 for the first book and $.50 for each additional book.

______ I prefer faster delivery to book rate. I am adding $2.50 *per book* for Airmail.